STORIES FROM THE ANDES

FREDERICO LARA WILSON

STORIES FROM THE ANDES

Frederico Lara Wilson

https://www.escapingculture.com

Paperback ISBN: 979-8-9889527-0-1
Hardcover ISBN: 979-8-9889527-2-5
eBook ISBN: 979-8-9889527-1-8

Library of Congress Number: 2023915377

DEDICATION

To all my Hispanic-Latino & Indigenous
brothers and sisters.

Photo credit, Tariq Safieh

ACKNOWLEDGEMENTS

I warmly thank my immediate family—my wife, Mary Ellen Wilson, son, Gabriel Wilson, siblings, nephews, and nieces for their unwavering support and understanding during the completion of this project. I also extend my gratitude to Bill Marquez, Alfonso Zamorano, Congressman Raul Grijalva (D-AZ 7th District), lifelong Latino and Indigenous brothers and activists, and the Pascua Yaqui Tribe of Arizona. Their lifelong friendship, association, shared cultural consciousness, influence, and the family's thoughtful inquiries, comments, valuable critiques, and constant encouragement were essential to completing the work.

I especially want to thank ***Mayfly Design and Publishing Services***, whose expert book design and creativity significantly improved the consistency of this project. The publication, which is a result of our collective efforts, would not have been possible without the support and work of *Julie and Ryan Scheife and Jess LaGreca*, who helped me with page layout concepts, typesetting, printing, and eBook registration and publishing services. Your commitment and help were instrumental in bringing this work to the printing stage, and I am deeply appreciative of the significant role you played in this project.

Mayfly Design
1011 Washington Ave. S, Ste. 302
Minneapolis, MN 55415
(612) 801-4533
https://mayflydesign.com
julie@mayflydesign.com

Book Cover - Catalina Carrasco, Portfolio: http://catalinacarrasco.com

DISCLAIMER

Photo credit, Tariq Safieh

EXPLORE

As a general rule, I don't give advice. But on one particular occasion, I counseled my nephew at a low point when he felt lost and sought guidance and the strength to carry on.

"Where do I draw strength?" he asked. First, I replied, "Fold your arms across your chest and hug (love) yourself. Are you done? Good, now let's move on. In no particular order: take inventory of yourself and your situation, and own it. Pick up the pieces. Sooner rather than later. There's a world out there waiting for you. Yes, you. You're in demand. You'll discover new people, relationships, perspectives, and *cultures*. You'll find that new places and people are pure entertainment and enlightenment. Laugh with and not at them. It's free. And that's something when you mistakenly believe you have nothing. Now, go explore. When you get bored, explore some more. Incrementally, things will fall into place. Trust me, nephew. I've been there, done that. You can do that too. Love you. Now, stop hugging yourself. It's creepy."

. . .

To readers of this book, his story is your story, too. We all feel lost at times. Find strength in exploration. Our individual story, our journey of discovery, is about human experiences shared outside boundaries, real or imagined. It's about purpose, center, role, and place in life.

EVERY STORY MATTERS

Stories vary and make us unique.
They're a birthright
rooted in
biography, biology, and geography.
When shared,
our life experiences transport us.
Journey to Cuenca, Ecuador,
the gateway to the Andes.

Stories hold a profound significance in our lives, transcending boundaries and touching the depths of the human condition. They are a powerful source of inspiration and connection, reminding us that each individual's experiences and emotions are essential in this vast tapestry of existence. Every person craves acknowledgment, a deep-seated desire to be heard and seen. At the heart of this yearning lies the essential need for a witness who can empathize with and appreciate our unique narratives.

The beauty of stories lies in their universal appeal. They resonate with people from all walks of life, transcending cultural, language, and geographical barriers. By offering a glimpse into the lives of others, stories foster empathy, un-derstanding, and a sense of shared humanity. Regardless of our background or upbringing, we all find solace and mean-ing in stories that reflect our joys, struggles, and triumphs.

Contrary to popular belief, creativity is not limited to a select few; it resides within each of us. We are all innately creative beings capable of weaving compelling tales. Stories provide a canvas for self-expression, allow-ing individuals to channel their thoughts, dreams, and emotions into narratives that impact storytellers and au-diences. Embracing our creative selves nurtures a culture of inclusivity where every voice finds its place.

In the rich tapestry of life, *stories are the thread that binds us.* Every story deserves to be told and listened to with respect and openness. Sharing stories fosters an atmosphere of acceptance and understanding, opening the door to myriad perspectives that enrich our collective consciousness. Embracing diverse narratives promotes a sense of unity. It helps dismantle barriers that often divide us.

Stories have a transformative power that can lead to healing and catharsis. They provide a safe space for individuals to confront their deepest fears, regrets, and trauma. By sharing their vulnerabilities, people find solace in the solidarity of others who have faced similar challenges. Witnessing and being witnessed in this healing process is an invaluable part of the human experience.

By acknowledging that every story matters, we celebrate the diversity of human experiences and promote an inclusive world where all voices are recognized, heard, and seen. Let us embrace our innate creativity and use the power of storytelling to foster respect, understanding, and compassion for one another as we navigate the intricacies of life's grand narrative.

TABLE OF CONTENTS

FOREWORD

This book defies traditional genre categorization. Rather than fitting into one specific genre, it is a collection of observations woven into postmodern narratives that touch on multiculturalism, untold stories, and images. In other words, it's a layered composition—literary Jazz.

Just as jazz musicians work with established chord progressions and melodies but add their unique interpretations and improvisations, I began with a free-flowing theme and images from which to build unexpected discoveries and fresh perspectives. This approach provided a foundation to build upon, allowing for spontaneous responses, leading to unanticipated exploration in uncharted territory.

Commentary has been added to provide context to the stories. Singular narratives, as expressed by individuals in the book, don't always capture nor should they differentiate cultural norms that provide personal and emotional truths when compared. As the author, that's my job, and that's my interpretive writing style.

The stories in this book are told through a multiethnic lens, with narratives that vary in language, chronology, and commentary—best understood by those open to multitasking narratives to better gain a robust understanding of the connections and nuances between people and cultures. Through this approach, I aim to provide a more engaging and holistic experience for the reader.

If you're accustomed to traditional Western publishing genres, you may find 'Stories from the Andes' unconventional. Its innovative work requires an open mind and a willingness to explore new perspectives.

For me, improvisation is the heartbeat of writing. Like jazz, it brings energy, creativity, and life to the written word. When I allowed myself to take risks and improvise, I discovered new possibilities in my work.

I hope you enjoy reading 'Stories from the Andes' as much as I wanted to write it. If you're open to new ideas and perspectives, you'll find it a rewarding experience.

PREFACE

Latin America's history is replete with diverse cultural, social, and political movements that have shaped the region's identity. Yet, these stories are frequently absent from mainstream discussions within the American narrative. From the struggles for independence and the legacies of colonialism to the impact of dictatorships and the fight for human rights, Latin American history is rich with tales of resilience, resistance, and sociopolitical transformation.

The history of U.S. involvement in Latin America, including political interventions, economic exploitation, and cultural exchanges, has profoundly impacted the region. However, these complexities are rarely explored or acknowledged in mainstream America or, by extension, their 'Western-thinking' cousins.

Latin America's countries and cultures have rich histories, traditions, and struggles—Ecuador is no exception. Ecuador boasts a wealth of cultural heritage that is often overlooked. Embracing and celebrating its cultural mosaic would enrich the American narrative and foster greater cross-cultural understanding. It is essential to actively seek out and promote Latin American voices, stories, and contributions to help bridge gaps and foster mutual respect between the North and its southern neighbors.

All individuals have a narrative rooted in their biography, biology, and geography. However, unfortunately, the majority of stories told and heard are centered on North America and Europe. Consequently, societal narratives have transformed over time into myths.

Throughout history, mythmakers have derived power from the condescension within the stories they tell themselves and others within their sphere of influence. Like all mythologies, these stories can be twisted to convey benevolence or malicious lies disguised as truth. Fortunately, South American stories that have yet to be told are gradually emerging. The more stories we hear, the more we can learn. While our cultures differ, our unique stories can unite us.

As an independent publication, the Escaping Culture book series aims to challenge the false narrative about Latin America that has persisted for too long. As the founder and editor, I strive to tell untold stories from Latin America, a term that encompasses South America, Central America, Mexico, and the Caribbean but also acknowledges the uniqueness of each country.

Anthropologists and sociologists recognize the importance of stories in providing historical context for a country's culture and people. However, when left to outsiders' interpretation, culture can become distorted, debased, and devalued.

It's important to acknowledge that Latin American countries are diverse and defined not only by language or culture but also by their borders and historical experience. Nevertheless, they are often subjected to an exaggerated sense of Western cultural superiority, which views them as "inferior" and unworthy of intellectual consideration and respect.

This falsehood persists because of narratives that promote and preserve the fallacy of Northern and European preeminence and dismissive and contemptuous behavior towards other countries and cultures. These storylines are based on high expectations of the West and low expectations of foreigners, creating self-fulfilling prophecies that reinforce the belief in the inferiority of others. This phenomenon leads to a person's or group's expectation of the behavior of another, bringing about the prophesied or expected behavior.[1]

It is essential to acknowledge that fabricated stories can alter reality if people believe them and they spread. In this case, a deliberately dishonest account has impacted the relationship between the North and South.

As honest arbiters, we must acknowledge history. Latin American countries are rich in natural resources. Still, their people have been exploited and remain poor due to despotic governments and global financial oligarchies that have taken advantage of their power to extend their control. They have taken everything: the petroleum, the timber, the fish, the hemp, the cocoa, the coffee, the rubber, the bananas, the rum, the gold, the silver, the copper, the diamonds, the tin, the lithium, the hydropower, and cheap labor. Latin America has been exploited for centuries and is not inherently poor and underdeveloped.

Confronted with these realities in a polarized world, building sustainable personal relationships free from state media narrative and governance outside our control is essential. To do so, we must first *escape our own culture and explore* to understand other cultural perspectives and perceptions.

A short monologue expands on this assertion of life, sustainability, and survival, albeit analogously. Sir Richard Attenborough, the renowned biologist and natural historian, affirms in a short BBC documentary called "The Miracle of Hatching."[2]

(Paraphrased and edited for brevity).

"An egg (culture), whatever its shape, is an excellent life support system. But paradoxically, its success will ultimately depend on the ease with which it can be broken. The time comes when a chick must break free. Some species invest time building up large yokes, and their chicks will emerge. Fully feathered and ready to search for food. Others have not made that investment. They will have to spend energy feeding naked and defenseless chicks over the next few weeks.

1. [Self-Fulfilling Prophecy R. Rosenthal, in Encyclopedia of Human Behavior (Second Edition), 2012]
2. [The Egg: Life's Perfect Invention | About | Nature | PBS. https://www.pbs.org/wnet/nature/the-egg-lifes-perfect-invention-about/17191/]

Furthermore, he opines, "Eggs are a perfect life support system . . . and today there are still hundreds that have never even been described." But how does the (chick) escape from the cramped confines of the egg? How could the shell that's been strong enough to protect the chick from the outside world be weak enough to allow the chick to break it? There's still much magic and mystery to escape and explore."

Given this context, each culture is an ancestral incubator, birthing fledglings into fiercely competitive social environments. Unsurprisingly, Ecuadorian stories were born in a volcanic cauldron, full of disorder, redemption, and a flourishing modern resurrection. Each account is a uniquely human experience with circumstances, characters, events, and opinions that interest someone *if told and heard*.

Throughout our lives, we have an obligation to seek enlightenment outside the margins of prevailing social attitudes and conventions. The truth is that it's different for everyone, and some may never do it, but the power to shape our awareness and character is within our reach.

Peer-to-peer, face-to-face engagement is critical in changing the world individually. It is an antidote to the hierarchical power brokers whose tenure as masters of the world has wrought social, economic, and environmental catastrophe and is bringing us dangerously close to extinction. By sharing multifaceted Latin American stories and viewpoints, we can foster and shape Ecuadorian perspectives and provide a larger frame of reference for others worldwide to consider and contemplate.

We must act to expand our international social awareness and understand people different from ourselves. For the past twenty-five years, I've traveled throughout South America and recently to Santa Ana de Los Cuatro Rios de Cuenca, commonly called Cuenca, the capital and largest city of the Azuay Province of Ecuador. Located in the Andes Mountains highlands, 8400 feet above sea level, it has a metropolitan area population of 700,000 inhabitants. Traveling and breaking free from the nationalistic narrative allowed me to bridge the cultural divide and broaden my understanding of others.

It's hard not to love Ecuador's most charming city. Its cobblestone streets, old-world cathedrals, colonial parks, and urban rivers make it a picturesque destination. The city is a melting pot of cultures, languages, and traditions. The Quechua, Canari, Kichwa, and many other indigenous groups, including the Siona, Secoya, Cofan, Shuar, Zaparo, and Huaorani, have managed to preserve their identities despite centuries of conquest by the Inca, the Spanish, local elites, and foreign corporations. The city's beauty and natural surroundings have also attracted many expats seeking a better quality of life and year-round spring weather.

Every country has an authoritarian element embedded in its political and economic system, and Ecuador is no exception. The government has suffered under the rule of dictators and oligarchies primarily controlled by U.S. and Canadian corporate interests. Ecuador's society could be better, and it continues to face challenges as it strives to meet the demands of a rapidly growing population. Thousands of Ecuadorians emigrate annually to escape the country's complex political and economic circumstances. However, those fortunate enough to have work and the support of family and friends manage to persevere in the face of hardship. The city's beautiful surroundings—emerald mountains, rivers, parks, and volcanic lakes—offer sanctuary to those who seek it.

I interviewed people from all walks of life in this cradle of contradictions. The conversations were a reflection of a society that is undergoing a socio-economic awakening and grappling with the uncertainties that come with it. Young and old, rich and working class, shared their individual stories, interwoven into a tapestry of civilizations and geography.

These stories are linked and supported by excerpts from former observations and compositions. They illustrate that individual stories shared are truths that can connect us emotionally and intellectually regardless of place and time.

The book provides context and perspective and bridges the discussions. It includes photographs and commentary in notes, remarks, observations, and annotations.

PRIMER

A primer is necessary to appreciate and grasp Ecuador's distinctive nature fully. Like the stories of its people, Ecuador is deeply rooted in geography, biology, and biography. To truly understand this country, one must become acquainted with its diverse landscape and delve into its rich history, from the pre-Spanish epoch to the Colonial period, the early National era, and the tumultuous political events that have shaped Ecuador throughout the 20th and 21st centuries. While Ecuador boasts 47 volcanoes, the symbolic 48th geographic rivalry best defines the challenging environment in which its people are born and forced to navigate to survive and prosper.

Photo credit, Frederico Wilson

Before the Spanish arrived, archaeologists discovered ceramic antiquities from 3000 to 2500 BCE. These communal remnants are considered some of the earliest in the New World, and their artistic traditions and artifacts influenced cultures ranging from Peru to Mexico.

By the 15th century, regional populations in Ecuador thrived through agricultural cultivation and trade routes that extended from the Pacific to the Andean Sierra and the Oriente, which encompasses the eastern Andes region and stretches into the lowlands of the Amazon basin.

The Inca conquest of Ecuador began with Peruvian tribal chief Topa Inca Yupanqui (1471-93), who introduced the Quechuan language into what would later become Ecuadorian territories. As the primary language of the Inca Empire emanating from the Peruvian Andes, Quichua is considered the most widely spoken pre-Columbian indigenous language in the Americas.

By 1532, the Spanish, led by Francisco Pizarro, initiated their conquest of the Inca Empire and systematically repressed and destroyed virtually every aspect of

Inca culture by 1572. Having conquered the Inca, the Spanish turned their attention to Ecuador. Spanish occupation in the 16th and 17th centuries fueled the disunity and chaotic relationships among Ecuadorians today, stretching from the Pacific Ocean to the Sierras and the Amazon basin.

During the colonization of the Sierras, Catholic doctrines indoctrinated the indigenous, forcing them to abandon native cultures and to onerous textile labor and indentured servitude. Coastal populations, on the other hand, were decimated by diseases introduced by the Spanish, and they remained largely abandoned until the advent of modern medicine. However, small populations of mixed ethnicities, including enslaved people, free black individuals, indigenous peoples, and mestizos, engaged in fishing, shipbuilding, and cocoa exporting from the port of Guayaquil. This coastal development represented a distinct cultural development separate from the Sierra. In the Amazon basin, the Spanish Jesuits evangelized the Quichuan language and the Catholic religion to subjugate and further indoctrinate the local populations.

The first Ecuadorian rebellion against the Spanish occurred in 1809 in Quito. In 1822, the South American liberating armies of Venezuelans Simon Bolivar and Antonio Jose de Sucre came to the aid of Ecuadorian rebels from neighboring Colombia. On May 24th, in a decisive battle near Quito in Pichincha mountainous terrain, Sucre defeated the Spanish, guaranteeing Ecuadorian independence.

After gaining independence from Spain, Ecuador briefly joined the confederation of Gran Colombia, which comprised Panama, Venezuela, Colombia, and Ecuador. However, on May 13th, 1830, after prolonged and contentious provincial differences, Ecuador seceded and became an independent republic.

Over the next century, Ecuador experienced a period of foreign occupation and internal strife, causing the country to turn inward. Ethnic, economic class and political rivalries emerged, each vying for control over labor, land, exports, and government management. Throughout the mid-20th century, a series of authoritarian regimes held power, with the military exerting a prominent and conspicuous influence over Ecuadorian governance.

In 1941, due to territorial disputes, a war erupted between Ecuador and Peru, which was eventually resolved in 1998. During the 1970s, the economy experienced a boost from petroleum profits. However, the economy suffered greatly when oil prices plummeted in the 1980s. This downturn led to political chaos and social unrest throughout the 1990s. To alleviate the crisis in 2000, the local currency, the Sucre, was replaced by the U.S. dollar.

Political parties in Ecuador are primarily organized along geographic lines and derive their power from specific regions, professional classes, and ethnicities. In the wealthier areas of the Sierra, moderate political parties dominate, and their influence extends to government employees and the educated professional classes. Conversely, the more progressive and left-leaning political parties are primarily centered in Quito, the capital city, as well as in Loja and the poorer northern and central highlands. In the coastal regions, power resides among proletarian organizations and movements with increasing indigenous participation. Since no single political party holds power throughout the country, coalition building becomes crucial for maintaining political leverage and authority.

Despite its politically chaotic history, internal divisions, instances of indigenous rights abuse, and socioeconomic inequality between the rich and poor, Ecuador remarkably managed to flourish when compared to other Latin American countries.

CATALINA'S STORY
LIVING IN CREATION

Art elevates our collective consciousness above the social order.

Catalina Carrasco's enigmatic origins and extraordinary talents evoke the notion of a time traveler, seeded in the 18th Century Enlightenment era. With an unbiased perspective on life reminiscent of great thinkers such as Voltaire and Rousseau, Catalina's philosophical nature challenges conventional ideas and invites contemplation.

As mere mortals bound by earthly realities, we are privileged to witness the ethereal journey of gifted individuals like Catalina, who defy dimensions, space, and time, morphing into transcendent couriers through their artistic endeavors, primarily through painting, destined to inspire and enlighten.

Her connection with the 19th-century Impressionism art movement, embodied by luminaries such as Manet, Monet, and Renoir, suggests a transcendental relationship to that era. However, she does not confine herself to a single genre but evolves and develops her unique painting style.

To better understand Catalina's artistic expression, I invite you to explore the links at the back of this book, which showcase her exceptional talent and creativity. Beyond painting, Catalina's explorations led her to various other creative pursuits, including theater, musical

Painting credit, Catalina Carrasco

composition, dance, and photography. These diverse endeavors expand her artistic horizons, demonstrating her commitment to continuous growth and evolution. Ultimately, her journey brings her to the 21st Century in Cuenca, Ecuador, where she currently resides amidst the solitude of the Andes Mountains.

In her secluded sanctuary, Catalina's artistic pursuits persistently elevate the collective consciousness of humanity. Guided by her belief in equality, knowledge, freedom, and love, she endeavors to heal the transgressions of humankind through her travels and art. This noble pursuit of inspiring transformation and positive change resonates with the core of her being. It remains a driving force throughout her existence, whether on Earth or elsewhere.

The epoch of the 'Age of Carrasco' defies time constraints. Catalina's creations and teachings possess a prophetic quality that will grow in value over time. Through her art, she transcends societal norms. She invites us to embrace a higher consciousness, elevating our collective awareness. Catalina Carrasco's extraordinary journey is a testament to art's power to inspire, enlighten, and shape our world perception. As we delve into her story, let us be captivated by the timeless significance of her contributions and their enduring impact on future generations.

Painting credit, Catalina Carrasco

CATALINA CARRASCO

INTERVIEW

The interview was conducted in English and Spanish at Catalina Carrasco's painting studio. It has been reconstructed from notes, audio text, translations, and recollections of conversations and edited to augment clarity.

[Interview Abbreviations: CC, Catalina Carrasco; FW, Frederico Wilson]

FW: Catalina, First of all, thank you for having us. Let me begin the interview by telling you a little bit about ourselves. As a publishing company, stories are the best way for people worldwide to connect on a human level. That's why we wanted to talk with you and allow you to discuss your life journey, philosophies, and artistry.

Let's begin with Cuenca.

CC: Well, this is my family home. It's extraordinary because of the mixture of people that live here. The indigenous, Spanish, and European combinations, their ancestral heritage, going back to the Inca.

When the Spanish arrived, they conquered the Incas and other indigenous people in the region. Tragically, they destroyed native cultures and local knowledge. Before they came, Cuenca was wonderful, and it was called

Photo credit, Catalina Carrasco

El Valle de las Flores (Valley of the Flowers). This valley, with its four rivers, was a paradise.

In many ways, the Spanish were arrogant and ignorant. They brought with them Catholicism, and they dismissed local spiritual ceremonies and customs. Many people in Ecuador are trying to resurrect indigenous culture and rituals again. It's difficult because several generations of people in Ecuador were and are influenced by Western culture and Western thinking. Western culture is a hybrid of superficial thoughts. The language can be cold and impersonal, and the people seem empty, like zombies. It's very sad.

FW: Being of mixed ethnicities, Pascua Yaqui Indian, Mexican, and White, I can relate. Many indigenous tribes and Latinos in the States feel the same way. They've paid a high price to be assimilated.

CC: Yes. Especially here in Cuenca in the 80s. We wanted to be like people in the United States and Europe. It's funny because people from the United States don't think of "America" as Latin America or South America. It's very strange to me. When I worked in Florida around 1983, I was talking to a lawyer, and he asked me, "Catalina, where are you from?" And I said, "I'm from South America." And he answered, "Oh wow. So you're from Texas."

FW: En serio? (Seriously?)

CC: En serio. (Laughing)

FW: (Shaking my head) It's hard to believe sometimes, right?

CC: It's bizarre, it's like our continent doesn't exist.

FW: Well, that's the narrative we're trying to change.

CC: There are so many tales to be told. About family, the beauty of people, small towns, and people of different faces and mixtures. And of course about the natural beauty of the country. I love Cuenca and the freedom of the countryside.

FW: I noticed on the drive up here that there were a lot of old abandoned houses in the countryside.

CC: Yes, a lot of the poor abandoned the houses. The Spanish white people, through land grants, owned most of the land. They didn't think the Indians deserved to own land, and they would make the Indians work it.

FW: So it was a feudal system.

CC: Yes. Yes. The Indians could only work the land, not own it. They didn't have the power. They were not considered citizens. They were just like the black slaves in the United States. The Spanish tried to kill most of the Indians in South America. Sometimes, they used to cut their hands off when the Indians did something they didn't like.

FW: The brutality of man is incomprehensible. The Belgians did the same to the people of the Congo.[1]

CC: The system remained the same until 1918. Prominent Spanish families were very, very wealthy. A lot of the poor had to leave the country to escape. You can understand why the indigenous and the poor grew up with resentment and anger.

FW: Indians were banished from their own country, others lived as exiles inside the country.

---

1. *In the period from 1885 to 1908, atrocities, including the amputation of hands, were perpetrated on the people of the Congo under the rule of King Leopold II of the Belgians. These atrocities and resulting genocide were associated with the labor policies used to collect natural rubber for export. Wikipedia.org/wiki/Atrocities_in_the_Congo_Free_State*

CC: Yes, that's right, like reservations in the United States. They were treated like animals. The Church and the Priests owned much of the land and used it for slavery. There's a very dark history about the Spanish, the Church, land use and distribution in the countryside, and the indigenous people that live here.

My great-grandfather used to be one of the people who owned many lands. But he was a humanitarian and one of the first landowners to help the indigenous here. The people loved him, and he owned La Quinta Guadalupe. My great-grandmother learned Kichwa, and she used to support the indigenous women.

FW: So your family lived among the indigenous? What are their origins?

CC: My family migrated from Italy and France, bringing a love of art, music, and people.

FW: So it runs in the family?

CC: Yes, I think it's in the genes.

FW: Are we in your family home?

CC: Well, no. I built this home in 2010, and we have other family homes in this area.

FW: You built it? It's beautiful. Peaceful. In nature. Perfect for an artist.

CC: Yes, perfect for my son, Sebastian, and me. He's 21. Sadly, he's suffered and endured much in life. He was born with Goldenhar Syndrome.[2]

FW: I'm sorry, I'm not familiar with the condition.

CC: He was born in 2001. We don't know for sure,

Photo credit, Catalina Carrasco

but we suspect the cause may have been the U.S. and Ecuador spreading poison to kill the cocoa plants.

FW: We've had similar crop poison cases in the United States. A weed killer called Roundup is suspected of causing all kinds of cancers. I also remember Parathion, a pesticide used for spraying crops in the fields, being banned.

CC: As a mother, I asked about the cause. Because I was a painter, they said maybe it was caused by paint toxins. I felt guilty, but other doctors said it was caused by family genes. Then, I discovered that many people using it in their gardens also had children with the same condition. It's been hard, and he's had 10 surgeries.

---

2. [*Goldenhar syndrome is a rare suspected congenital condition characterized by abnormal eye, ear, and spine development. The origin is unknown at this time. Most cases of Goldenhar syndrome occur in families with no history of the disorder. —Children's Hospital of Philadelphia, chop.edu*]

FW: So brave. Can we meet him?

CC: Yes, he's upstairs and kind of shy. Maybe later.

FW: And how is he doing?

CC: Good. Well, you know, it was not easy for us. I divorced 12 years ago. I had to support my son alone. It was tough because making a living as an artist is difficult. I was teaching at the University, but the government changed the teaching credentials to teach. At the time, I had to have what you in the United States called an undergraduate degree. When Rafael Correa became President, they changed the teaching requirements. You had to have a superior certification—like a Master's degree to teach. I also worked for the Cuenca municipality as a photographer. The man I won't name in the Culture of Ministry took that job away. So that was also difficult. But I kept this piece of land to build my house. So now my son is by my side, and we have security. He's fine now. We're doing well, but it took work.

FW: How long have you been making a living as an artist?

CC: Over 40 years.

FW: I couldn't believe the number of paintings in your catalog. You must be working all the time.

CC: Yes. I love what I do. It's a blessing to love art and to be in touch with my family and the environment. It's a gift.

FW: As is your imagination. It shows in your paintings. Einstein once said that logic will get you from point A to point B, but imagination will take you everywhere. When did you know as a child that your imagination would take you to art? Did you know that art was going to be your calling?

CC: It was early. My Mom said I always liked to express myself and perform in front of her friends as a child. I remember feeling an adrenalin rush. But now, as an adult, I'm super shy and feel better alone in my studio. It's tough to even go to my exhibitions, and I have to force myself. At the shows, they see me through my pictures—and then they see me. People you don't know will walk up and want to talk to you.

FW: At the Munay exhibition, I noticed your body language and how you reacted when people approached you. They wanted to hold you — a part of you.

CC: Yes, it's uncomfortable, but I understand. It's the commercial part of the business.

Painting credit, Catalina Carrasco

FW: It was interesting how people matched themselves to particular paintings and saw themselves in them. We loved the show.

CC: Yes, that happens often. The show went well.

FW: I noticed different musical instruments in the house. I know early in life, you expressed yourself through dance and throughout your life through painting. Do you also compose music?

CC: Yes, I play the guitar and sing. I used to be in a band.

FW: So throughout your life, you've lived in creation—through different mediums. Given that, let me pivot to a philosophical question. How would you compare who you were as a creative person to who you are now and who you may become?

CC: Wow! That's an interesting question. It's a never-ending process. A continuation of work. All art is energy, for example, music. Musical vibrations transcend language and travel. In these mountains, you hear music from the valley below every Saturday. It makes this place magical. People here are very religious; they play traditional Christmas music and songs around Christmas. It's beautiful. You hear it coming from the valleys, mountains, and churches all over Cuenca. You wake up in the morning with music and listen to it all day. It happens throughout December. People love celebrating Christmas, preparing for big parades, and rejoicing in the baby Jesus all year.

FW: Spirituality is very much a cornerstone of the culture here.

CC: Especially in music and song.

FW: We know you've traveled. I've always said that the most exciting culture is the one I'm off to see next. There's always something new to discover. The more you see, the more your appetite is heightened. I see exploration in your paintings, which take me to real and imagined places. Tell us about your travels and how it's influenced your paintings.

CC: When I was a young girl, I lived in Paris. A bizarre thing happened when I was in a square in the 9th District. A man came to me and asked me to perform. I asked him what this was all about, and he said, "You have to destroy all the paintings and the sculptures of the artists participating in this exposition."

There were many children with hammers and sticks prepared to destroy everything. I didn't know what to do. I found out that the curator had planned all of this. It was a statement about the rejection of contemporary art. This was back in 1974, right? Everybody was against it back then because art wasn't seen as relevant. Things like a window with some junk on top of it. So they wanted to destroy it to make a statement. At the time, I thought he was crazy, but now I think he was brilliant. I should have taken the hammer and broken everything.

FW: (Laughing) And how old were you?

CC: I was eight years old. I'm 54 now, and I finally understand what the curator was trying to tell the children. *Create something new with soul*, not just a shoe with a hole in the middle and a bunch of text inside the hole to explain what it means.

FW: I noticed that symbolically, you're in many of

your paintings. Jackson Pollack once said he had to be inside his paintings to fully experience[3] the piece.

FW: In distinctive ways, you share the need to 'live' inside paintings to fully express yourselves. So you continue to explore other cultures?

CC: I travel and explore a lot, but not because I have a lot of money. First of all, I am fortunate.[4]

CC: I was born into a family that traveled around the world. Also, as an artist, people from different countries invite me to stay in beautiful places to show my art. These opportunities are one of the reasons I decided to become a professional artist. It's been a wonderful experience. As I mentioned earlier, my initial travel experience was to France. The second was to Spain, and the third was to the United States, where my father was a teacher. He taught in Lexington, Kentucky. For me, it was a new and wonderful time. I love country music and dance, and I have a lot of good memories of the Southern culture.

FW: Country, jazz, or blues. Depending on what part of the South. We lived in Memphis for 15 years.

CC: Yes, I was there.

FW: When Elvis Presley was alive?

CC: Yes. And I missed the concert because my brother was very young and there was no nanny to care for him then. I was very young, around nine years old. I knew Elvis would have a concert and we had a good friend who could help us when we arrived. He was a scriptwriter for the Pink Panther movies. My brothers and I stayed in his house and went to school there.

FW: How many brothers do you have?

CC: I have two brothers, and they are both cinematographers. Rafael was born in Spain shortly after El Franquismo,[5] which I'm sure you know was a dictator—a Catholic religious authoritarian.

CC: So, yeah, we were in Spain at that time. We then went to the United States and stayed at our friend's place, which I mentioned earlier. Funny story. He had a radio station. While we were there, he went to Japan for the holidays. He was a practical joker. Unknown to us, he had told his audience to call in and speak to extra-terrestrial beings. Of course, nobody in our family spoke English. He connected all the phones to the radio, and every time someone would call in, we used to answer in Spanish. I remember my father answering the phone once, and the

---

3. [My painting does not come from the easel. I prefer to tack the outstretched canvas to the hard wall or the floor. I need the resistance of a hard surface. On the floor, I am more at ease. I feel nearer, more part of the painting, since this way I can walk around it, work the four sides and literally be in the painting." —Jackson Pollack, American drip painter and a major figure in the abstract expressionist movement].

4. [Upon hearing how 'fortunate' Catalina was, I recalled a CBS interview with Pete Kadens, a Chicago millionaire who retired at 40. He and fellow entrepreneur Ted Koenig founded the Hope Chicago Program, which covers post-secondary credential costs (college, trade schools, etc.) for 30,000 Chicago area students and families. His comments continue to resonate. He opined, "I'm a guy who got really lucky in life. I'm a guy who won a lot of lotteries: the birth lottery, the zip code lottery, and the education lottery. And when I think about having won all those lotteries and all the people suffering, it's my chance to give them those same opportunities. That's who I am. This is my life's work. This is what I'm going to spend the rest of my days doing because I believe that I was put on this earth to enable other people to get the same opportunity and access that I have."—Opportunities, Chicago scholarships]

5. [Francisco Franco was a general and the leader of the Nationalist forces that overthrew the Spanish democratic republic in the Spanish Civil War (1936–39); thereafter, he was the head of the government of Spain until 1973 and the head of state until his death in 1975. —Britannica]

caller laughed at him, making him very angry. I thought it was hilarious. Our friend was a joker, lovely. We got our own house after staying with him for a short while. He helped us a lot when we were in the States.

FW: Is he still alive?

CC: I don't know. We lost track of him. We met so many incredible people when we were there. It was a beautiful time, you know? Especially for me at an early age. Then, I came back to Ecuador and attended a Catholic school. I was not too fond of school, but I had to do my studies. I was bullied and laughed at because I used to speak Spanish differently because of my European and United States experiences.

When I was 18, we returned to the United States to be with friends in Oakland and San Francisco, California, and I loved those places very much. I got a scholarship to Stanford, but it only paid 50%, and because it was so expensive, I still needed to finish. So, I left and went to work in Florida and traveled to Venezuela and Argentina. Then, I went back to Ecuador to finish university.

FW: You were on your own during this time?

CC: Yes. I was very independent.

FW: So you mentioned Mexico.

CC: Yes, I traveled to Mexico because my Father had art exhibitions there. I was in love with Mexico, especially Oaxaca. The colors, the people, and oh, the food.

FW: My roots are in Mexico, and my people are from Sonora and Sinaloa. In my former business, I traveled throughout the country. I share your feelings. Pivoting back to Ecuador, I understand you spent some time restoring murals around the city.

CC: Yes, I studied architectural restoration techniques. I helped restore the El Museo del Monasterio de las Conceptas.[6] (Museum of the Nuns). I assisted in restoring the murals and the pictures. I was twenty-two years old.

CC: It's a private place for nuns. Fascinating place. The nuns make a lot of sweets and food and sell them to the public to help fund the monastery. They're servants to the church, have a good heart, and are very innocent. They live a life of Namaste.[7] I wanted to be a nun when I was young and innocent. But I was instructed to meet a man and decide whether to join a monastery. Of course, I did meet a man and decided that life in a monastery was not for me. I am too curious by nature.

---

6. [*The Museum of the Monastery of Las Conceptas (Nuns) began in 1561 and has evolved into a museum of pictorial collections. After 40 years of the founding of Cuenca by the Spanish, a female cloister was required where the daughters or descendants of the conquerors could enter. Only in the 60s of the 20th century did these treasures begin to be exposed to the public since they remained out of sight by monastic orders. The Cloisters are open on the occasion of the IV National Eucharistic Congress, held in Cuenca in 1967. For the first time, the public from Cuenca and visitors from the outside can see and admire both the interior of the building and the collections that were kept there. However, at the end of the Congress, the monasteries closed their doors (with few exceptions). At the beginning of the 80s, a restoration project was finally generated in the monastery to turn it into a museum. The project was carried out by architects from Cuenca, Edmundo Iturralde, Gustavo Lorrelt, and Hernan Crespo Toral. With this project, the infirmary of the cloister was restored, which allowed the doors to be opened to Hermano Miguel Street, where it became a symbol of the city. The art collections became part of the museum's art collection, which continues to belong to the nuns but is not managed by them. —Wikipedia, Conceptas Monastery Museum—Conceptas Monastery Museum*]

7. [*Namaste is a Sanskrit phrase that means "I bow to you."—Equivalent of hello, but with an element of respect—NPR, Namaste*]

CC: I don't think you can be curious and devote yourself to service and prayer. Yes, life in a monastery is safe—but it's not free. I need the freedom to live. In a monastery, you can't laugh out loud. You cannot scream or dance, and you cannot express yourself. *And art is all about expression.*

FW: So this home has become your destination, your sanctuary? Is it by choice or chance?

CC: Well, both. My Mom and I were looking for a place. We were driving outside Tarqui and saw a sign, 'Land for Sale,' on the side of the road. We connected with the seller, and he gave us a reasonable price. With the help of my Father, we bought several parcels of land. My Father gifted me this parcel, and my brothers and Mother have other properties nearby. We built a family communal inside an indigenous community.

In the beginning, it was very hard to be accepted. The Indigenous don't trust strangers and are very careful about people who might change their culture. But we earned their trust by working with the community. In fact, my Mother taught English to the children. They 'tested' us for about *five years* before we were accepted.

Now people from different countries live up here. They're from Germany, Canada, and the United States. They all want and share the same things: safety, beauty, and peace. Everybody watches out for their neighbors.

FW: There's harmony and conflict to living here. I understand why you settled here as an artist. On the one hand, you sought safety, serenity, and sanctuary. On the other hand, your imagination is free to soar beyond boundaries and borders. Are you familiar with the story of Icarus?

CC: Greek mythology? Yes, I am.

FW: I'm curious: do you ever feel in your flights of imagination that you're in danger of flying too close to the sun and falling from the sky? Wasn't the moral of the story about balance? That life is a gift. And maintaining the distance between the sun and the ocean ensures long life.

CC: Yes, but more than that. Artists, by nature, are *unbalanced.* The moral of the story is also about pride and limitations. As artists, we explore beyond restrictions. I would fly directly toward the sun until I was tired and couldn't go any further. We sometimes fly too close to the sun and fall, but as artists, we continuously explore. It's in our nature.

FW: Point taken. So you live an unbalanced life.

CC: Yes, yes. (Smiling) it could be genetic. My Father and Mother are opposites, and I have both inside me. How do you say it? A dichotomy?

FW: Fascinating. Do you feel creative people have the same conflict?

CC: Most of us. Yes. We're thoughtful, curious, and always searching.

FW: Searching for (pausing) truth?

CC: Yes, always truth.

FW: Independent truth, an individual, subjective truth.

CC: Most of us have this imbalance. My paintings were always about truth, healing, and raising consciousness. Consciousness drives us, and that's why we need to do art.

As a child, I used art to escape my parent's troubled relationship. Both of them are artists. As children, my brothers and I had to choose between my father's 'hippie' art lifestyle and my mother's more traditional way of life. She was a ballet dancer and painter when she was younger. We chose to follow our mother. We used art to heal our pain. It was lifesaving.

[I shared Catalina's thoughts and feelings about the well-being art delivers, as expressed in one of my previous books—'The Reckoning.'][8]

Photo credit, Catalina Carrasco

CC: The world can be dark. Through crisis and chaos, we're drawn to light to heal. It's the source of multi-dimensional awareness and truth. It is a prayer, a garden where all living things unite. I don't like the word God. We prefer light as the source of healing energy.

FW: You see art as a bridge to higher consciousness.

CC: Artists serve as the conscience of people. Some people even consider us as shamans, connecting them to other dimensions.

FW: I think of your art as an expression of love. Whether earthly or in the dimensions of your imagination and paintings. I sincerely appreciate your letting us into your world and giving us your perceptions and artistic visions.

I'm sure you're familiar with Gabriel Garcia Marquez, author of 'One Hundred Years of Solitude.' In another novel, 'Love in the Time of Cholera' he may have expressed love the best.

---

8. *[Whether accentuating the beauty and fragility of the natural world or creating the imaginable by words, design, or construction—art elevates our collective consciousness above the social order. It resides within us. It lives, by extension, through our inherent need to create idiosyncratic expressions painted on canvas. It lives through a camera lens, capturing a revolutionary moment and through our adoration of exquisite sculpture. It lives in the elements of musical compositions and inside the covers of every book ever written. It lives in the fluidity and the grace of interpretive dance. It lives in the murals on city streets and concrete canvas. It lives in the shape of an earth-encrusted clay pot. It lives in vineyards, harvest, and wine cellars. It lives in culinary cuisine. It lives in the benevolent calling to watercolor a smiling child.*

Living in creation shields us from society's intrusiveness and emboldens us with self-respect and a sense of worth. The creative process frees us from the mundane and the ordinary and grapples with grief, mortality, and love. It grants us safe passage, hosts alternative realities and reason, provokes us to act, and, most importantly, gifts humanity, truth, and higher consciousness.

Art is our raison d'etre; it's our state of grace. It's our refuge and escape from the bombardment of cultural orthodoxy. It provides a safe harbor and connection to all who seek it. It revives our senses, strength, inspiration, and imagination. And best of all—we need only to look inside ourselves to discover it.]

"Over the years, they both reached the same wise conclusion by different paths. It was impossible to live together in any other way or love in any other way. And nothing in this world was more difficult than love."

CC: Yes, love is a difficult path. But it's the only path.

FW: Yes, indeed. Thank you, Catalina, for sharing your love with the rest of us.

POSTSCRIPT

In many ways, I share Catalina's viewpoints. A few closing thoughts.

In this unparalleled period in human history, the masses are increasingly disillusioned, growing hostile, going hungry, and becoming racially and socially polarized. The predatory body politic is the source of this empirical lunacy rules with cash and guns without mercy and morality. ART, our lifeline, has nearly been abandoned. It's become a commodification of culture, bereft of philosophy, social value, and the human condition. We're at a precipice, about to take a permanent step that commits us to existence or extinction.

Suppose we're to survive as a species. In that case, we must escape the control of cult(ural) war, disease, famine, environmental degradation, and the cult of personality, leading us into 21st-century serfdom. At times, we're fighting against gravity itself. But fight, we must.

In interviewing Catalina, I purposely tried to go beyond my own life into the beliefs of others to help me navigate personal presumptions and propositions. Weaving through doubt and supposition, I understood that all stories are interconnected—and necessary to confront and challenge humanity's failed stewardship, governance, and alternative paths to happiness and survival.

Readers will appreciate Catalina's story and artistry as forms of expression that are intrinsically related, sister means of reflection and revelation.

PHOTOGRAPHS
THE CATALINA CARRASCO COLLECTION

All photograph were taken at Cotapamba Bajo, Parroquia Tarqui, and Azuay, Ecuador.

Todas las ilustraciones tienen la misma localización: Cotapamba Bajo, Parroquia Tarqui, Azuay, Ecuador.
Portfolio: http://CatalinaCarrasco.com
Email: KataCarrasco@gmail.com
WhatsApp: 0992149751
Cuenca, Ecuador

Catalina Carrasco

Catalina Carrasco

Catalina Carrasco

Catalina Barraco 2021

Catalina Carrasco

Catalina Carrasco

Catalina Carrasco

Catalina Carrasco

JUAN CARLOS SOLANO

STORYTELLER

"The best stories aren't written. They're eaten."

Gastronomy, in the hands of a storyteller, is literature on a plate. Culinary tales await you at Juan Carlos Solano's "Tiestos" Restaurant. The cuisine has an origin, theme, color, culture, and intrigue.

Chef Juan Carlos is an original. He is a man born of Ecuadorean earth, born to conceive food as art. He is intuitive to the values of the land, fauna, and environment. He is to the Cuenca Sierra what volcanos are to the inter-Andean region of Ecuador. He is authentic, commanding, and fiery.

Photo credit, Juan Carlos Solano

In gastronomy, where flavors dance and aromas captivate, there exist chefs whose passion for food is akin to an untamed fire, fueling their creative spirit and igniting their culinary journey. Among them stands Juan Carlos, whose unyielding dedication to culture, tradition, and the power of connection has set him ablaze, shaping him into a true culinary maestro.

Rooted in the rich tapestry of Ecuadorian heritage, Juan's love for his culture serves as the bedrock of his gastronomic identity. From the bustling markets to the remote villages, he seeks to uncover the hidden gems in traditional dishes. Inspired by his ancestors, he weaves stories and flavors together, crafting masterpieces that pay homage to the diverse regions of his beloved Sierra.

Every dish he creates is a canvas on which he paints a vivid picture of his country's past, present, and future. He conscientiously seeks out rare ingredients, unearthing the forgotten treasures of his culinary heritage. With each bite, diners embark on a sensory journey, discovering the essence of the land through its vibrant colors, bold spices, and textures.

No fire burns brighter than the love and support of family and friends. For Juan Carlos, they form an integral part of his culinary exploration. Their unwavering belief in his artistic talent fuels his talents. In the bustling kitchen of Tiestos, Juan Carlos is not a solitary flame but rather the focal point of a blazing inferno. His restaurant staff, a talented ensemble of chefs, waitstaff, and kitchen hands, work in synchrony, their collective passion and dedication radiating throughout the establishment.

Together, they create an environment where creativity flourishes, and culinary boundaries are pushed. Juan Carlos's leadership inspires his team to embrace innovation while staying true to the culinary traditions that have shaped them. Their collective fire transforms the restaurant into a haven of culinary excellence and heartfelt hospitality.

Beyond the flavors and aromas, he understands that food can unite individuals from diverse backgrounds. He's has transformed Tiestos into a communal table, and food becomes a vessel for storytelling, shared experiences, and cherished traditions. He creates a space through his dishes where people come together, forging deeper connections and lasting memories. He understands that food is nourishing for the body and a catalyst for human relationships and shared experiences. The smiles and satisfied palates of those who savor his creations are the ultimate rewards, fueling his passion for continuing to create culinary masterpieces that touch hearts and evoke emotions.

Juan Carlos embodies a culinary artist driven by an all-consuming fire, stoked by the love of culture and customs, family and friends' support, his staff's dedication, and his profound affection for people. His story is a captivating journey of an extraordinary chef whose flame is as fervent as the Ecuadorian sun.

Photo credit, Juan Carlos Solano

JUAN CARLOS SOLANO

INTERVIEW

Juan Carlos Solano's interview was conducted in English and Spanish at "Tiestos"—his authentic Ecuadorian restaurant. The interview has been reconstructed from notes, audio text, translations, and recollections of conversations and edited to augment clarity. Leonardo Duran (a native Cuencano), an associate of mine, joined us at the early morning meeting.

[Interview Abbreviations: JCS, Juan Carlos Solano; FLW, Frederico Lara Wilson; LD, Leonardo Duran.]

FLW: Juan Carlos, thank you first for agreeing to meet us this morning. As we explained earlier, we're an independent publishing company. We've become increasingly aware that most books about Cuenca are written by expats for expats. It was long overdue that Cuencanos had the opportunity to tell their stories and perspectives to the world. We wanted to discuss your restaurant, which symbolizes Cuencano culture. Let's begin with this magnificent building.

JCS: We're having coffee in a patrimonial house[1] built in 1890.

Photo Credit: Frederico Wilson

---

1. *[Patrimonial—inherited by established rules (usually legal rules) of descent; an ancestral home]*

Photo Credit, Leonardo Duran

FLW: Historical. Coffee tastes better here. It's beautiful. Kindly introduce yourself.

JCS: My name is Juan Carlos Solano Jaramillo. *Tiestos* is my restaurant. I was born and raised in Cuenca, Ecuador.

FLW: When I sent you an invitation to interview, I asked you to tell us about Cuenca and your personal story. Thank you for granting us the interview. How did you become a chef and owner of this restaurant?

JCS: It was never my idea to cook and open a restaurant. It was a matter of fate. My father owned an ice cream parlor shop. But, one day, he said to me, "This is my business; do you like it? If not, there's the door." He sent me out of the house. I stood, out in the street, "Son-of-a-bitch, I'm screwed." What do I do now? I'm not under my Mom's skirts anymore.

All: [Roaring laughter]

JCS: My father's best decision was to send me out of the house.

(Grinning) So now, I have to go find work. And I was big…big…I mean, really big. I weighed 340 lbs. So, because I was so big, I went to work as a nightclub guard.

FLW: When was this?

JCS: 2002.

[He pulls out a couple of photos. One where he weighed 340 lbs. The other was when he was much slimmer.]

FLW: When did you lose the weight? How did you lose so much weight so quickly?

JCS: From 2005 to 2006. With the help of my wife, I exercised and ate a healthy diet. I was diagnosed with pre-diabetes.

[Leonardo and I sit silently, dumbfounded at the change of his body transformation.]

FLW: Who taught you how to cook?

JCS: My mother. She's a great cook. I learned to mix flavors with her. What you eat here in the restaurant is different from book recipes. They are my family recipes. Then, I went to work at a friend's restaurant that sold guinea pigs, and at the same time, I studied cooking at the Chamber of Tourism. From there, I started working at different restaurants to gain more experience. Eventually, I opened my restaurant with a few tables in 2008 without advertising. The Americans would come to El Centro (downtown Cuenca), walk by, stick their heads into the restaurant, and ask, "Do you sell food?"

JCS: (Laughing): "Yes, of course, we sell food."

Americans: "What food do you sell?"

JCS: So I tell them authentic regional food. And when I was talking with them, I would let them taste some dishes.

Americans: (Animated, raising their arms) "Spectacular!"

JCS: They had never tasted my mixtures and mountain seasoning. Because nobody was doing (blends) what I was doing back then. The Americans loved it. They went and returned with friends . . . and they kept coming back.

FLW: All word of mouth?

JCS: Yes! The people of Cuenca who knew me from other restaurants where I worked previously began coming. I HAD SALES! I had 40 chairs and a line of people outside the door. Thank God!

So, at the same time, I went to the Center for the Promotion at the Chamber of Tourism. There was a French-man there; I think his name was Jack Terrier. He said, "Eating in the world today is the simplest thing. But making it memorable is up to you. When you set up a restaurant, you must make the food not only delicious—but unforgettable! You have to think about the atmosphere, the music, the service, and most importantly, the quality of the food you serve because that will permeate people's memories."

And that's what we've achieved. I specialize in local foods prepared with ingredients from this region. You want eating to be an experience. That's what many people in the restaurant business need to fully understand. I have people from different places in Ecuador who have been coming back for over 14 years.

FLW: A large part of the dining experience is the atmosphere, engaging customers, and the story behind the local food and ingredients. You're tapping into all human senses: taste, smell, hearing, touch, sight, and movement.

JCS: Of course.

FLW: Intriguing. You molded a unique cultural dining experience.

JCS: That's what we're trying to create. Food is psychological and a philosophy. If you look at gastronomy, you'll realize that minimalist designs (dishes) will comfort you.

FLW: The same could be said of all art. And food is an art form. Down-to-earth to esthetic?

JCS: In gastronomy, this is how I see the world today. (Mockingly) Pretty, cute, tall dishes with foam in the air. We forget about us, the people, and the purpose. We should remember the essence of food. *The heart of what it is to sit down to share.* We need to remember our neighbors. When you go home to eat, what do you expect? The food is in the middle of the table to share. You come back to the essence of what we are human beings. We're a cell of society. The family. That's what generates a community. We have to hold the family together. And food unites us. That's what gives us strength. That's what we try to do in this restaurant.

FLW: And what happens when customers do not engage with you?

JCS: Many people don't accept this, right? Accordingly, you have to know how to handle these scenarios. How do they let you into their circle? I make adaptations in the kitchen. The waiter will serve you the first dish and ask, "Can I bring you anything?"

For example, he will bring *traditional* salty food with sweet sauces that, in Ecuador, we call *lampreado*. It's a base of our food, a dish served for as long as that product is cultivated or over-cultivated within an area and that people still need to try to eat.

We also serve typical food dishes made out of potatoes and pork. So we adapt and serve typical and traditional dishes our customers are curious about to satisfy their tastes. They may not be familiar with them at first. But if they try them and are satisfied, they allow us into their circle, and we guide them into our *shared* family concept. When you eat pizza, don't you put it on the table, and everyone shares? This is the primary cell of society. Sharing makes the world a family.

FLW: Tell us about the theme and the origin of the restaurant.

JCS: You see, I grew up mostly with my grandparents. My mother's family spent nine months of the year in the city and three months in the country cultivating the fields, planting, and collecting. We would collect grains, herbs, corn, chili, beans, cheese, and other things. That was the food, right? So we grew up like that. The food we collected and ate that's the origin of a restaurant. The roots with which you grew up—the ingredients, the recipes, the flavors you make yourself, which you love are the ones that we use in this place.

FLW: Authentic mountain food. Did you know that "Tiestos," besides the pots you use to cook and serve food, means "love and lover"—and in other parts of the world, it means "God of trance?" So, you could say all these meanings directly or indirectly apply to the restaurant, que no?

JCS: (Asking LD): Que dice? (What did he say?)

FLW: (Amused) En serio (seriously).

LD: (Puzzled) I didn't know that.

FLW: Anyway, let's play a word game. I will give you a word, and I'd like you to respond with the first thing that comes to mind. Okay?

JCS: (Confidently) Okay.

FLW: Faith.

JCS: (Without hesitation) I put all my faith in my wife, daughters, and God. All my faith.

FLW: Of course. Beautiful. Besides the struggles in opening up a business, we all have to overcome things daily that affect our lives. Can you speak to that?

JCS: I could tell you that my struggles are all about the restaurant, but in all honesty, most of my struggles have been outside the restaurant.

FLW: Is it too personal to talk about?

JCS: Well, family comes first. The struggle is always to keep the family together. Not economically, but in personal ways.

[Juan Carlos pauses, collecting himself.]

JCS: There's a song by Javier Solis that says, "I have to laugh in front of people, but my heart is sad inside." Sometimes, I feel like that when working and talking to people at different tables. I have to pretend I'm happy and convey that happiness to my customers, like a double life. At times, I have to become Juan, the "dad"—Juan, the "husband"—Juan, the "cook," always cool. That's the toughest fight in the restaurant and in life. Always being positive and happy. *Sometimes, that's a struggle.*

FLW: Yes, juggling all the facets of life and business. Totally understand.

LD: Juan Carlos, tell us, who or what are the most significant influences in your life? It can be an event or person.

JCS: Two things made me what I am. My relationship with my father took me out of my comfort zone and made me enter the world. And my family, my wife and daughters. They are behind everything I do, my goals and aspirations.

I planned on having the best restaurant in Ecuador and having the same customers return year after year—I believe I have achieved that.

I had a goal many people set for themselves in the restaurant business: opening a restaurant chain. But that was not logical for me. Because I cannot divide my time. I can only adequately serve up to one location.

FLW: This is it, then. You're giving everything you have to this restaurant and the people you serve.

JCS: Todo (everything).

FLW: So, tell us about memorable characters in your life. Everybody has a crazy uncle.

JCS: [Laughing heartily] Yes, of course, everybody has a crazy uncle. I had a crazy uncle who I won't name. When we were children, he used to take us fishing. He would make us a tea with an infusion of herbs—and a little bit of alcohol. [He jumps from the table] "Let me make you a sample."

[He returns with a beautiful herb and flower concoction infused with unnamed alcohol.]

Photo credit, Frederico Wilson

[As he explained the ingredients (flowers, herbs, alcohol) and the distilling process of the drink, I asked him about any more memorable characters in life. I sip on the glass. I get an immediate rush. If I finish this, I'm in trouble. I nurse the remainder.]

JCS: A lot of memorable people have eaten here. Almost all of the artists who visit the city have eaten here. The President of the Republic, mayors, assemblymen, ministers. All the people in the government have eaten here. We have become an icon of the city.

Once, the Mayor of Manta and his entire entourage of councilors came here to eat and wanted pork and shellfish dishes prepared like they do on the coast. Well, they prepare food with different seasonings on the coast. I discussed it with him and prepared the dishes with mountain seasoning. In the end, (throwing his hands in the air) "Bravo," the Mayor said.

FLW: Admiring the drink presentation, I asked him, "What kind of flower is in the drink?"

JCS: Different flowers from the garden. It's a secret formula made from flowers people have forgotten. We distill it, add yeast, alter the aroma and flavor, and serve it on special occasions here or at home.

LD: This reminds me of when I was sick as a child, and my Mom used to give me different drinks made of flowers and herbs.

JCS: This is what I was talking about earlier: making food and drink memorable. I have customers, Cuencanos, Azuayos, and Canarejos, who left here for the United States, returned, and yearned for the food they remember growing up.

[Continuing with the word game and progressing on the drink but still coherent.]

FLW: So, Juan, what comes to mind when I say "purpose"—your purpose in life?

JCS: I want a dignified life—a dignified old age. You know, I don't want to be a hindrance to anyone. I want to have my own means of support. When I was a boy, the old people had to find somebody to welcome and support them: a son, a nephew, or a relative. They had to find somebody who could feed them. I don't want to be a burden to anybody. I don't want to ask for anything—not out of pride, but of dignity. I like that security for my wife and daughters. I want them to have a good life.

FLW: Hopefully, with good health and the restaurant's success, your concerns over time will subside. You know, everybody has deep-seated worries. What keeps you awake at night? What scares or worries you?

JCS: *Failure.* Not so much when I was younger, but it scares me now that I'm older. I must continue to make this restaurant successful to support my three loves: my wife and daughters.

FLW: Didn't skip a beat. Oh, you're good at this game. What makes you happy, Juan?

JCS: Sunday.

FLW: Day of rest and family?

JCS: Exactamente.

FLW: Regrets.

JCS: No remordimientos (regrets).

FLW: Somehow, I knew you'd say that.

[Curiously, virtually everyone I've interviewed in Cuenca has responded similarly. At the risk of overgeneralizing, Cuencanos simply don't internalize misgivings. It's not a luxury Ecuadorian life affords. They move on with their lives. Time is money. Life is short. It's part of a collective coping mechanism, coded into their cultural DNA.]

FLW: Let me switch the subject. What do you think of expatriates in Cuenca? This can be a touchy subject to both Cuencanos and gringos.

JCS: (Chuckling) I love them. They have influenced us Cuencanos so much that now we pick up the dog poop in the parks.

ALL: (Laugher)

FLW: Good for business?

JCS: Yes, of course.

FLW: What about happy, tragic, and tender moments in your life?

JCS: Tragic? Well, when my father died. It really hit us hard. Beautiful and tender? One particular Christmas when I was a child. My parents were very poor. They gave us a gift wrapped in newspaper. We kids didn't care about that; we only saw the gift. The gift was a very simple thing: a ball. I will never forget that day. It was very special, beautiful.

[Nodding collectively, we all pause for reflection.]

FLW: Gives meaning to "It's the thought that counts." Touching memory. Tell us about Cuenca. What makes Cuenca unique?

JCS: Cuencanos. I once heard a gringo talking to another gringo at the table, and he referenced Cuenca, that's stuck in my head. He was a gringo who lived here. The other came to visit him. The one who visited asks the one who lived here, "Why Cuenca?"

And the Cuencano gringo tells him, *"Cuenca is like a drop of fresh water in a salty ocean."*

FLW: That's a keeper.

JCS: You only know Cuenca once you touch it. After that, you don't want to leave. And if you think about it, it's very logical. Maybe I'm prejudiced, but Cuenca is not like other cities worldwide. The people from the North need help to understand. Please don't take that the wrong way. Look, I have gringo friends from the North who live in Cuenca, and we visit each other's homes. They are as "Cuencano" as any others. They have adapted to Cuenca; the city and culture are part of their lives. The hardest thing for gringos is learning the language. It's hard for people who don't adapt.

The world now knows Cuenca. To be honest, I don't like that so much. I'm jealous. I want to keep it like it is. We'll face technical difficulties like other big cities if we get much bigger. What do I want people to know about Cuenca?

Tell people, "Cuenca is beautiful, with beautiful people, and living here brings peace of mind."

FLW: Well, there's no better way to end this interview. Juan Carlos, thank you for taking time out of your busy schedule to sit with us for this interview.

[Levantándonos de la mesa, nos damos la mano y Juan Carlos me abraza—Rising from the table, we shake hands, and Juan Carlos hugs me].

FLW: (Jestingly) I'll take this drink with me, okay?

JCS: (Grinning, knowing it's knocked me on my butt) It's been my pleasure.

POSTSCRIPT

My wife Mary and I frequented *Tiestos* several days later. Juan Carlos, the artist, came to our table and, with assorted condiments in hand, drew an awe-inspiring welcome to us on a plate. Indeed, it is a dining experience—worthy of all our senses.

Photo credit, Frederico Wilson

DAVID FAJARDO'S STORY—
HUMAN RIGHTS, ENVIRONMENTAL LAWYER

"I knew when the great guiding spirit cleaves humanity into two antagonistic halves,
I would be with the people. I know this. I see it printed in the night sky."
—*Ernesto Che Guevara*

After meeting David Fajardo Torres, my memory was jogged with a timeless Native American folk story about an old chieftain schooling his tribe about the battle within each of us.

As the tale goes, the chieftain gathers his people around him and instructs them about the battle between two wolves living inside each of them.

One wolf is evil. It is anger, envy, jealousy, sorrow, and regret. It is greed, arrogance, fear, self-pity, guilt, resentment, inferiority, lies, false pride, and ego.

The other wolf is good. It is joy, peace, love, hope, serenity, humility, kindness, perseverance, and benevolence: empathy, generosity, truth, compassion, and faith in the spirits and Mother Earth.

Photo credit, Frederico Wilson

Photo Credit, David Fajardo

Photo credit, David Fajardo

casually drop lines from T.S. Eliot's poetry just as easily as he referenced Salvador Allende, the democratically elected Chilean Socialist President who was assassinated in a U.S. backed neoliberal military coup. Our conversations spanned various topics, from environmental and cultural perspectives of Alexander von Humboldt, the renowned 19th-century Prussian naturalist and explorer, to proto-socialist thinkers like Franco-Swiss philosopher Jean-Jacques Rousseau. Rousseau had argued for a re-evaluation of the social order, a notion that influenced the French Revolution and development of socialist and democratic theories.

With a solid educational foundation and philosophical clarity, David sought justice through his travels, indigenous rights battles, and Kuska Estudio Juridico, a progressive law firm in Cuenca, Ecuador, specializing in the rights of the disenfranchised, exploited, and marginalized.

David's advocacy includes supporting the Indigenous people and nationalities of Ecuador in their fight for territory, education, and cultural identity. He also champions the fundamental objectives of labor groups, students, and unemployed organizations staging anti-government protests and massive national mobilizations. Furthermore he actively supports the Steven Donziger Defense Fund,[1] which seeks to hold Chevron accountable for deliberately dumping billions of gallons of toxic oil waste onto ancestral lands from 1964 to 1992.

In deference, the assembled sit obediently, reflecting on the elder's word, until the youngest boldly stands and asks the chief, "Which wolf wins the battle?"

To which the sage replied, "The one you feed."

Instantly, I understood that David, an Ecuadorian human rights and environmental lawyer, like tribal members of the folktale above, reflected on his inner wolf. And that the "good wolf" steered him to a life altering journey towards justice, conscience, certainty, and morality.

The person seated across from me could have walked out of a novel. A young man so self-assured that he could

---

1. In 1993, Ecuador's Frente de Defensa de la Amazonia (FDA), representing 30,000 victims of Chevron's toxic oil waste, asked attorney Steven Donziger to help them win compensation for what is likely the largest oil-related human disaster in history. Donziger and the FDA legal team won the largest court judgment in history for human rights and environmental violations, a $9.5 billion verdict against the Chevron Corporation. Following this verdict, Chevron sold their assets in Ecuador and fled the country- Rex Weyler "The Man who stood up to an oil giant and paid the price" https://www.greenpeace.org/international/story/

Whether he is advocating for human rights, trekking through the jungle, scaling volcanic peaks, or sailing at sea, David immerses himself in the people, the land, the animals, and the culture he encounters. He perceives connections where others might only see differences. For David, everything is connected, and his life's purpose is unmistakable: to defend Mother Earth and its protectors. This philosophy is a calling that no government or corporate force can compromise.

While I cannot be sure if parallel universes or heavens exist or possess any intrinsic meaning or principles, I recognize a purposeful life when I see it. I marvel at David's deep compassion for the common good—a compassion that he extends for the betterment of us all. This is undoubtedly what David stands for. His dedication to environmental and human rights is admirable. He has set a bar so high that few of us will ever reach it. However,

it's worth striving for, and it commands both aspiration and admiration.

More often than not, many of us lead our daily lives in a bubble of self-absorption. It is incumbent upon us to summon our inner wolves and uncover our reserves of self-awareness and benevolence. If we do, we might discover that introspection and life itself are the greatest gift of all.

David's journey of self-discovery is a poetic tale of solidarity and finding one's place in the world. His life has been shaped by nature, academic teachings, classic and contemporary revolutionary philosophers, and family mentors, all of which have influence his perspective on people, politics, policies, and human and environmental rights.

Bravo, David Fajardo Torres.

POSTSCRIPT

I believe providence and misfortune wage a constant battle in our lives, with the winner ultimately determining our time on earth. Why, where, and when they come calling is a mystery. Not to put too fine a point into this, but fate led me to David. Stay with me.

While researching people to interview for this book, I came across David's name on LinkedIn, listed as an environmental attorney in Ecuador. I later made arrangements to meet with him upon my arrival in Ecuador.

In an earlier work and before arriving in Cuenca, I had written about the timeless Native American folk

story about an old chieftain gathering his people around him and instructing them about the battle between *two wolves* living inside each of them.

Fast forward, Mary, my wife, David, and I were seated at a local restaurant. I had the opportunity to show him a draft of his story and interview. To our astonishment, David unbuttons his shirt, and wolves are tattooed on each side of his chest. Now, call me crazy, but providence just came calling.

I don't believe science, nor does secular philosophy, or religion hold the answers to the mystery of why we're here, where we go, and what lies ahead. Some things are meant to remain unknown; perhaps an ambiguity insulates us from ourselves, from our inability to cope with revelations we're ill-prepared to handle. In the interim, we muddle through, hoping that revelation from whatever source provides clues to our pursuit of reason.

Do I believe we were destined to meet? *Damn straight*. As it turns out, I know precious little about providence and chance. I roll with it. We share David's love of nature and his mission to protect the environment and support the indigenous. That's reason enough for Mary and me to set up a foundation to help support David's environmental and human rights advocacy.

DAVID FAJARDO

INTERVIEW

We had the good fortune of interviewing David Fajardo on separate occasions at Jodoco's Belgium Bistro in San Sebastian Square and Café Del Museo, Calle Paseo Tres de Noviembre, Cuenca. The interviews provided insights into David's love, perceptions of nature, and human rights advocacy. David was one of the principal organizers of Indigenous and environmental activists who put a landmark referendum on the ballot to safeguard the biodiverse Yasuni National Park territory in the Ecuadorian Amazon from State and Oil drilling. The Yasuni area is unique in its richness of plant, amphibian, bird, and mammal species. It provides the highest levels of biodiversity per square meter in the world. By some estimates, over 150 threatened species reside there. The referendum's impact has the potential to shape a global precedent for direct democracy on climate change. Specifics to this momentous global environmental victory follow this introductory interview. The discussions were conducted in English and Spanish, consolidated, and edited for clarity.

[Interview abbreviations: DFT, David Fajardo Torres; FLW, Frederico Lara Wilson; MEW, Mary Ellen Wilson]

FLW: David, thank you for agreeing to meet us. I look forward to speaking with you because of your human rights and environmental advocacy. Both Mary and I are what Americans would describe as "tree huggers." Mary was raised in nature, on a farm, and my affinity for nature began with ecology courses in high school

Photo credit, David Fajardo Torres

and progressed while in the United States Air Force, monitoring environmental health and safety protocols. As ethnically mixed, white, Mexican, and Pascua Yaqui Native American, I am especially curious about your work with the Indigenous peoples in Ecuador, especially in the Amazon.

FLW: We understand you're an attorney and graduated from the University of Cuenca. What are your current pursuits?

DFT: I'm pursuing my Master's in The Rights of Nature at Universidad Andina Simón Bolívar in Quito, Ecuador. It's the only Master's degree that exists on the rights of nature in the world. The reason I studied law is precisely to be able to defend nature and the environment. It's challenging and complicated.

FLW: How old are you? Were you born in Cuenca?

DFT: I'm 29. I was born in Cuenca, but my mother's family is from an area called Victoria del Portete, which is outside of Cuenca. It is a rural area but quite close. It is a short distance, a maximum half-hour drive from Tarqui. That area is unique because it is where a metallic mining project tries to exploit gold. There has also been a lot of resistance from communities because the mining in the area will end the paramo.[1] This ecosystem allows rivers like the Tarqui River to exist.

My family is from Victoria Del Portete, which has generated a strong bond. However, I've traveled primarily for activism in and out of the country. My life project, at least in the short and medium term, is here in Cuenca and Ecuador—saving the paramo and working in the Amazon against mining and oil projects. My objective is to achieve a genuine ecological transition in the country.

MEW: Where does your love of nature come from?

DFT: That isn't easy to say, but it was very early. I felt this sensitivity towards non-human animals, trees, and plants. When I was a child, I lived in an area that, at that time, was peripheral to Cuenca; therefore, it was an area where you could still find many things of nature. So, I always remember that when I was very young, I would play in large tracts of land without construction, and we could still find it.

I would see many things: owls, tarantulas, spiders, toads & frogs. I would find tadpoles in puddles, and I felt sorry for them because I knew they would be run over by vehicles passing by. I would take a bucket and take all the tadpoles to my house and keep them until they became frogs, and then I would release them.

I loved doing that, but my grandmother and my aunts were afraid of toads—but I had to do it. I did the same with rats.

MEW: Rats?!

DFT: I would find them wounded in the streets. I felt sorry for them. I felt their pain. I thought I had to take them home to cure them until it was time to release them. So, at a very young age, I felt sensitivity to non-humans—which I now claim as normal.

---

1. *The paramo is a unique ecosystem dominated by giant rosette plants, shrubs, and bunch-grasses. It has fascinated scientists since Alexander von Humboldt visited them more than 200 years ago. They are a vital water source and a carbon sink that combats climate change. They feed streams, rivers, aquifers, and water catchment areas.*

MEW: Empathy.

DFT: Through Buddhist philosophy, I understood a lot about empathy. But we can talk about more philosophical questions after a few beers.

ALL: [Laugh]

DFT: My ecological identity was built at an early age.

FLW: How would you describe yourself now?

DFT: I would describe myself as an environmentalist—an Ecologist lawyer. I chose the law as a tool to fight for ecology, wildlife, and the rights of nature and Indigenous people. In reality, the law is a valuable tool to defend nature's rights, and we're now seeing a strong current of lawyers emerging.

FLW: I'm sure you're familiar with the Chevron case and Steven Donziger and the FDA legal team, who won the most significant court judgment in history for human rights and environmental violations.[2]

DFT: Yes, of course, he, along with Pablo Fajardo (no relation), set a critical precedent for other struggles to continue in the Amazon against oil and in favor of the rights of the communities.

He interviewed me when I was 18, maybe 19 years old. I participated in the campaigns and sent letters of support. Chevron started a powerful movement to extract oil from the territories. But there's a strong movement in the Ecuadorian Amazon to get oil companies out of the region.

DFT: Going back to your question about identity construction, my family has greatly influenced me. For example, when I was very young, my grandmother told me that before plucking a flower from a plant, I had to ask it for permission because it has feelings. It hurts when you pluck a leaf or a flower.

MEW: So you had to ask permission from the flower? Did you have to thank them?

DFT: Yes, I believe that to be true. And science has confirmed that about plants. The vast majority of plants have at least twenty-one senses. Humans, what, seven senses? And that kind of thing allowed me to grow. People grow up with a paradigm called Anthropocentrism[3], where the human is the center of everything. The plants, the animals, the rivers, the mountains, the soils, and the air are only important because they are helpful for human life. The non-human is as essential as the human. That is the great challenge we have as humanity: the importance of co-existence.

My mother and two grandmothers have greatly influenced me. My grandfather influenced me politically.

---

2. In 1993, Ecuador's Frente de Defensa de la Amazonia (FDA), representing 30,000 victims of Chevron's toxic oil waste, asked attorney Steven Donziger to help them win compensation for what is likely the largest oil-related human disaster in history. Donziger and the FDA legal team won the largest court judgment in history for human rights and environmental violations, a $9.5 billion verdict against the Chevron Corporation. Following this verdict, Chevron sold their assets in Ecuador and fled the country- Rex Weyler "The Man who stood up to an oil giant and paid the price" https://www.greenpeace.org/international/story/

3. Anthropocentrism means human-centered, but in its most relevant philosophical form, it is the ethical belief that humans alone possess intrinsic value. From an anthropocentric position, humans possess direct moral standing because they are ends in and of themselves; other things (individual living beings, systems) are means to human ends. —Science Direct—L. Goralnik, M.P. Nelson, Encyclopedia of Applied Ethics (Second Edition, 2012).

Little by little, I'm following the script. These influences and professional training have materialized into what I do every day. I owe a lot to my family. My family and culture are my foundation. I travel back to Victoria Del Portete[4] often to visit my grandparents. We're very close.

And I owe a lot to the geography where I lived as a child. The river has greatly influenced me. It's a very defining element in my life. My mother and grandmother's teachings about respecting nature, animals, and plants influenced me to stop eating meat at eleven.

I have an aunt, Patricia Torres, nine years older than me. We got along like brother and sister, not like aunt and nephew. We were having lunch (meat) and arguing about dinosaurs. She knew I had tried not eating meat when I was younger. I ate a lot of meat. I liked it. I tried at seven to stop and again at nine, but the temptation was too much. But at age eleven, I decided to stop because my aunt told me, and I'll never forget it, "If you care so much about animals, why are you eating one?" I didn't stop eating meat because I didn't like it anymore but because another human being felt like me. She decided to stop eating meat because of the mistreatment she saw of animals. It was like a blow to my face. That's when I decided I would never eat meat again.

Then there's the issue of cows.

FLW: Cows?

DFT: I always speak of cows when asked about vegetarianism. Did you know cows are so sensitive that they have 'best friends'? If the cow is separated from its best friend, it enters a state of depression, much like human beings.

MEW: We had cows on the farm, and that's true.

DFT: And what do cows and cattle eat? Soybeans. In turn, harvesting it in South America generates high rates of deforestation. There is a big problem in Paraguay, Bolivia, Argentina, and Brazil. And here in Ecuador, the Amazon is deforested to generate pastures so the cows can feed themselves. The Amazon forest is cut down. The issue of meat production, at a global level, is one of the primary sources of greenhouse gas emissions.

Indeed, one of the solutions to climate change, especially the dimensions of greenhouse gases produced by fossil fuels, is to change gasoline cars to electric cars. But this requires context. The truth is that the production of electric vehicles is very polluting because they need lithium batteries. There are very few places, for example, in South America, where there is a lot of lithium. It's primarily between Bolivia, Argentina, and Chile. And lithium extraction generates a lot of pollution. The truth is that the solution to the energy problem of transport for all people is the private vehicle: fewer vehicles, more efficient public transport. In Cuenca, we are doing our best. But we need to do more. We have efficient electric public transportation like the Tram.

[It should be noted that David arrived at the meeting on his bike.]

FLW: So, connect the dots for me. We are witnessing climate change driven by fossil fuels at an alarming rate. We all can do our part by not contributing to its escalation, but what do you see on a macro level as the root cause of our failure as a species to combat environmental

---

4. *Victoria Del Portete is a town and parish in Cuenca Canton, Azuay Province, Ecuador*

Photo credit, Carlos Alberto Iglesias Cabrera

degradation? Is the root cause the Capitalistic profit over people system?

DFT: Capitalism forces us to think of ourselves as individuals.* When in reality, we are collective societies. The human being is a collaborative social species. We cannot survive as individuals. Capitalism makes us think otherwise.

FLW: Are there other options in Ecuador?

DFT: There's cooperatives and communitarianism. Communitarianism effectively says that local territories can self-administer, that is, to be sovereign and decide for themselves the common good. That's what we're trying to do in Cuenca regarding mining. We reject the National Government of Ecuador's decision that Cuenca has to be a mining territory and, therefore, a region of ecological sacrifice. We, in Cuenca, agreed that this territory is for conserving the nature of water and generating environmental policies.

FW*[I agree that we're a collaborative species. Still, individuals have a responsibility to change the world. I completely agree with David that options other than (crony) Capitalism must be explored. But I don't believe in the binary systems, Capitalism vs. Socialism. Both systems must be updated to keep up with technology and ever-changing geopolitical events. New hybrid economic strategies must be explored to shift power from shareholders to stakeholders. A form of this is taking place in China. Yes, China. Xi Jinping, China's President, is using the stock market to serve the public sectors of the State, like infrastructure investments and social welfare and prosperity programs (education, environment, health, etc.). He's redirecting capital flows to bolster the economy, control corporate power, and turn capital to serve his people over corporate profits.

Additionally, Chinese regulators are empowered to restrict capital extraction, i.e., company insiders from selling their shares if their company's shares fall below their issue price or if it fails to pay dividends to its shareholders. Companies have to pay if they seek entry into the enormous Chinese market. The experimental hybrid system allows for the power of market fundamentals to play out while simultaneously preventing the capitalistic capture of the economy.

Having said this, there may be more realistic options for Ecuador, given the political climate, but that's another discussion for another time. I mention this only to contextualize the Capitalism Socialism references in the interview.]

FLW: Allow me to change the subject. Tell us about some memorable characters in your life.

DFT: The Crocodile Hunter.

ALL: (Laughter).

DFT: Yeah, Steve Irwin[5], the "Crocodile Hunter." I used to watch his documentaries on TV when I was a kid. I was fascinated. I loved seeing how he worked with animals like crocodiles and told you about his life and why defending and protecting them was essential.

I was also fascinated by another person, Jane Goodall[6], and her defense of chimpanzees and gorillas. When I was six, my mother gifted me a National Geographic magazine. Jane Goodall spoke about illegal hunting. My plan as a child was to study biology and veterinary medicine. I also wanted to become a photographer for National Geographic, making a living out of traveling the world and taking photographs. That was my plan until I was 16 years old.

MEW: What changed?

DFT: My goals changed. I got interested in astronomy. Galaxies fascinated me. I studied at a very religious Catholic school, Puente Coliclo Borja. It's a private school for boys in the Banos district of Cuenca. They taught you everything related to religion. But I began to question religion a lot because they taught us that God had created nature and animals for us to take advantage of them indiscriminately—as if they were merely tools, valuable elements, nothing more. For me, that kind of thinking was very limiting. Critical thinking, scientific thinking, and even logical thinking were not allowed. That's when I decided to become an atheist, but I continue to be spiritual. Let me explain.

DFT: As a child, we do things that captivate us.

MEW: Curiosity.

DFT: Exactly. We're interested because we're curious. We try things. We experiment. As a result of the experimentation, we generate knowledge, which we then share. So all children are scientists at the start. Unfortunately, the educational system indoctrinates you to stop thinking. The result is a child who consumes ideas rather than one who generates them. I accepted spirituality. I applied it to my relationship with all things that surround me. For example, I connect spiritually with non-human things, like a river.

FLW: The otherworldly feeling we experience gazing at the ocean or a sunset.

DFT: Yes, it goes beyond the teachings I was experiencing at school then. Spirituality is the relationship between people and nature. It's essential to have an open mind and a critical mind. Preventing people from thinking critically is part of the goals of people who have accu-

---

5. Steve Irwin was an Australian zookeeper, conservationist, television personality, wildlife educator, and environmentalist. In 2006, he died from an injury caused by a stingray while filming an underwater documentary on the Great Barrier Reef. —Wikipedia

6. Dame Jane Morris Goodall is an English primatologist and anthropologist. She's considered the world's foremost expert on chimpanzees after 60 years of studying wild chimpanzees' social and family interactions. —Wikipedia

mulated much power and want things to continue. That is to say, there is a ruling and exploited class. When an exploited class thinks critically, it rises and demands that things change. This is precisely what is happening now as it relates to people wanting an ecological transformation away from fossil fuels and more to renewable energy.

I have recently enjoyed getting to know Humboldt[7] more closely.

He traveled from the top of Chimborazo[8] to the depths of the Amazon. He led a fascinating life. He wrote extensively about the relationship between nature and human beings. He's known for being the father of geography. He was the first ecologist in history.

Humboldt was a great inspiration to a young Charles Darwin.[9] They should both be read in a historical context. Darwin defended racism in his publications on competition and natural selection. He was very controversial. Within the evolutionary process, he came to support that there are superior human races, specifically that whites were superior to people of African descent—wrong on so many levels.

And then there's another giant source of great inspiration to me, Pyotr Alexeyevich Kropotkin[10], a Russian revolutionary and geographer. He challenged the Darwinian principle that evolution was strictly about the survival of the strongest. He thought that cooperation rather than conflict and competition is the chief factor in the development of species.

He acknowledged that competition was a factor in the evolutionary process, as did mutualism and symbiosis.[11]

For example, birds feed on the parasites of rhinoceros. The rhinoceros benefits, as do the birds. Mutualism. They help each other in the evolutionary process. Mutual beneficial relationships can be built socially and politically. Darwin promoted individualism, while Kropotkin promoted collectivism. These ideas clash. We have to strengthen the collective. Suppose we believe that competition defines our social relations. In that case, we're destined to think there will always be winners and losers.

Most importantly, we educate the masses about nature and everything in it. We have to have empathy. It is our great responsibility.

FLW: What drives you now and in the future—educating the masses?

DFT: Yes, educating the masses and fighting for these transformations. Knowing that more and more people are fighting to change the world would make me very happy.

MEW: And what makes you unhappy? There are times in our lives that make us sad when we reflect on that.

7. *Alexander von Humboldt (German geographer and naturalist)*
8. *Chimborazo is an inactive stratovolcano (20,548 ft. elevation) situated in the Cordillera Occidental range of the Andes. —Wikipedia*
9. *Charles Darwin (1809-1882) English naturalist, geologist, and biologist—Theory of evolution by natural selection/On the Origin of Species, 1859*
10. *Kropotkin thought that sociability is a dominant feature at every level of the animal world. Among humans, too, he found that mutual aid has been the rule rather than the exception. —Britannica*
11. *The interaction between two different living organisms living in close physical association, typically to the advantage of both. —Oxford Dictionary*

DFT: A sorrowful moment was when my fellow activists were murdered. Andres Durazno[12], a partner of mine in the struggle, was one of the prominent leaders in Rio Blanco. We know who the culprit—the murderer was. He's on the run. It's personal. Mining alters the social relations of the communities.

FLW: Does it all come down to sovereignty and extracting a country's natural resources?

DFT: That's a very complex issue. I will answer concretely. Natural resources are common goods. For example, water belongs to humans and all other species. The forest needs water. Animals, plants, and insects all need water.

FLW: A distinction not accepted by a profit-motivated capitalistic system.

DFT: It's the imperialist way of doing things. The real solution should be cooperation, not domination. I reference a favorite living philosopher and sociologist when exploring alternative approaches to societal disputes and resolutions. His name is Boaventura de Sousa Santos.[13] He's the Director Emeritus of the Centre of Social Studies at the University of Coimbra, Portugal. He's regarded as one of the world's most prominent epistemologists and left-wing intellectuals.

FLW: Help me out here. Epistemology, as I under-

---

12. *Business & Human Rights Resource Centre—Article, March 24, 2021- Environmental activist and human rights defender Andrés Durazno was murdered with several stab wounds outside his home in Llantahuayco (Azuay) on the night of Tuesday, March 17, 2021. This was announced by the Allianz of Human Rights Organizations [Alianza de Organizaciones por los Derechos Humanos], a coalition of almost twenty social organizations, through a press release . . . Durazno was president of the community's water and irrigation system of Molleturo-Río Blanco. This is a rural parish located west of Cuenca on the edge of the Cajas National Park. Since the arrival of Ecuagoldmining South America S.A., a subsidiary of the Chinese company Junefield Mineral Resources Holdings Limited, the community of Río Blanco has been involved in several conflicts over access to water sources for its inhabitants, animals, and crops.- https://www.business-humanrights.org/en/latest-news/ecuador-asesinan-a-defensor-del-agua-y-opositor-de-la-miner%C3%ADa-en-r%C3%ADo-blanco/*

Mongabay.com Series Report by Kimberley Brown, July 9, 2021: A new report by Ecuador's Alliance for Human Rights examines abuses against environmental rights defenders over the past 10 years and finds 449 defenders subjected to intimidation, threats, harassment, persecution, and assassination. The report concludes that not only has the Ecuadoran State failed to protect rights defenders, but it has also been directly responsible for some of the abuses, like the concerning number of persecutions and prosecutions of rights defenders. Three environmental rights defenders have been murdered in Ecuador over the past 10 years—Andres Durazno, Freddy Taish, and Jose Tendetza—with no one brought to justice for the crimes.- https://news.mongabay.com/2021/07/environmental-defenders-in-ecuador-arent-safe-new-report-shows/

Land is Life.org—October 27, 2022—Land is Life Condemns the Murder of Alba Bermeo Puin, Indigenous Defender and Anti-Mining Activist in Ecuador: Alba Bermeo Puin, a 24-year-old Indigenous defender and anti-mining activist, was murdered on the night of October 21 by people associated with illegal mining in the communities of Rio Blanco, Cochapamba and Yumate. She was five months pregnant. According to human rights organizations and local Indigenous associations, the murder is affiliated with an unprecedented escalation of threats and violent attacks against community leaders opposing mining activities in their territories. —https://www.landislife.org/land-is-life-condemns-the-murder-of-alba-bermeo-puin-indigenous-defender-and-anti-mining-activist-in-ecuador-1305/

13. *According to Global Social Theory, Sousa Santos's greatest contribution to social theory is recognizing plural epistemologies (a branch of philosophy concerned with knowledge) and systems. Sousa advocates local solutions rather than ‹hegemonic globalization narratives, which tend to favor Western perspectives. Santos characterizes Western European epistemologies as ‹abyssal' in that they make a sharp distinction between their way of thinking, presented as correct, and all others, such that other ways of knowing cannot find recognition or be present in the production of knowledge.*

stand it, includes philosophers like Plato, Descartes, and virtually all great thinkers throughout history.

DFT: It's a philosophy about the origin of knowledge and the study of nature and rational thought.

FLW: Well, no one is going to accuse you of not being well-read.

DFT: (Grinning) I'm enjoying this conversation very much.

FLW: Let's turn our attention to Cuenca. What makes Cuenca unique?

DFT: If something makes Cuenca unique and special, it is the rivers, the Tomebamba, Yanuncay, Tarqui, Machangara, and Norcay. In a referendum[14] in February of 2021, Cuenca voted against mining and extractivism that would have endangered the rivers and drinking water[15] of Cuenca.

FLW: Definitely. I've traveled throughout Latin America, and potable water was always an issue. So you're continuing your water activism here in Cuenca?

DFT: I am. I belong to a couple of organizations. One is Yas Unidos Cuenca, and the other is Cabildo for the Water of Cuenca.

DFT: Part of the identity of people from Cuenca are the rivers. Suppose you ask anybody from Cuenca what the most beautiful thing about Cuenca is. In that case, they will say either the rivers—or the Cajas Mountains. People from the North need to understand our relationship with nature. That's why we have a solid movement to oppose oil and mining exploitation. We intend to build an economic model on nature conservation and scientific tourism. Scientists from all over the world come here to investigate our biodiversity without threatening it or destroying it.

MEW: So, what do you want people to know about Cuenca?

DFT: I want people to know that Cuenca decided to protect the rivers and the environment. Like I said, it's part of our identity.

FLW: Any last thoughts?

DFT: I am working with the Schwar people, an isolated indigenous in the south Amazon, fighting Canadian mining companies. I work with the CONAIE[16], Ecuador's largest indigenous rights organization. I am also working with the Yasuni indigenous communities fighting to remove the oil companies from their territories.

FLW: I would love to interview indigenous leaders. Can you arrange that?

DFT: With pleasure. Please listen to their stories.

---

14. *"It was the first time in Latin American history that a binding referendum against large-scale mining is won in a big urban city."—Maristella Svampa, Argentinian sociologist—Cadtm.org*

15. *Drinking Water Filtered by the Cajas Mountains—Una Nueva Vida—A New Life by Stephen Vargha, Excerpt: "The Cajas (mountains) is like a giant sponge. The volcanic soil on top of the rocky surface absorbs much of the water that falls from the sky. Once saturated, the water heads towards Cuenca . . . the filtered water is clean and crystal clear. To some expats, the water reminds them of the great tap water enjoyed in Seattle and western Washington."*

16. *Confederation of Indigenous Nationalities of Ecuador—CONAIE represents the following indigenous peoples: Shuar, Achuar, Siona, Secoya, Cofan, Huaorani, Zaparo, Chachi, Tsachila, Awa, Epera, Manta, Wancavilca, and Quichua.*

FLW: That's what it's all about. I look forward to it.

MEW: No, we look forward to it. I'm going, too.

DFT: (Laughing) Of course.

FLW: Thank you, David. We look forward to talking to you about the *Yasuni* court decision.

DAVID FAJARDO INTERVIEW

ECUADORIAN AMAZON OIL DRILLING
YASUNI NATIONAL PARK REFERENDUM

The Yasuni interview is a continued conversation with David Fajardo on the landmark referendum to safeguard the biodiverse Yasuni National Park territory in the Ecuadorian Amazon from State and Oil drilling. The discussions were conducted in English and Spanish, consolidated, and edited for clarity.

[Interview abbreviations: DFT, David Fajardo Torres; FLW, Frederico Lara Wilson]

FLW: I'm aware that back in 2008, Ecuador became the first country to grant *nature rights* in its Constitution, but how did grassroots Indigenous and environmental activists manage to put a referendum on the ballot to safeguard the biodiverse Yasuni National Park from oil drilling? How did you manage to bypass the political extraction interests in Ecuador?

DFT: It is necessary to start by indicating that the Constitution of Ecuador does not grant rights to Nature. What happens is that the Constitution develops, above all, a new critical paradigm that recognizes (knows again) Nature no longer as an object but as a subject. Therefore, its intrinsic value does not depend on appreciation and human valuation. The subject's rights, Nature or Pacha Mama, are recognized based on that.

FLW: Was the referendum a new strategy for indigenous and environmental rights activists?

DFT: Indeed, it was the first time that citizens proposed holding a Popular Consultation at the national level to stop the development of oil exploitation in the Ecuadorian Amazon.

FLW: So, I understand that the State has denied local communities the right to prevent oil drilling in the region for decades. Does the referendum give affected provinces safety, health, and security from big oil interests into the future?

Photo credit, Martin Zinclair

DFT: That's right, the decision to exploit oil in the territories of the Amazonian communities has always been a decision in which these communities have not participated but rather an imposition from the State and oil interests. By itself, the Popular Consultation on Yasuní has not meant more significant guarantees of safety or health since the consultation is specific to oil exploitation in Oil Block 43 within Yasuní. However, the State should understand this as the manifestation of the citizens' will to prioritize other issues over oil exploitation, such as precisely, safety and health, two public policies from which communities affected by oil have historically been excluded. Regarding protection against oil interests, it is necessary to emphasize that the Popular Consultation is binding and immediately compliant. Hence, its results are mandatory for the Ecuadorian State and other actors, including oil companies.

FLW: Do you have any estimates on reducing greenhouse gasses released into the atmosphere by keeping the oil in the ground?

DFT: According to some experts on the subject, such as Carlos Larrea, professor at the Simón Bolívar Andean University, Ecuador, by not exploiting the oil from Yasuní block 43, the emission of 407 million tons of CO_2 into the atmosphere was avoided. Although the extraction of this oil could not be prevented from the beginning, we managed to stop it in time to prevent most of these tons from being released into the atmosphere.

FLW: People would be interested in knowing that since the 1950s, missionaries allegedly have collaborated with oil companies, specifically Shell Oil, to displace Amazon communities from traditional territories. Can you speak to that?

DFT: Of course, especially evangelical missions like those of the Summer Institute of Linguistics, an evangelical Christian organization in the United States that, it is now known, was financed mainly by private individuals such as the Rockefeller family, prominent oil magnates, and the government of the United States. The purpose of the SIL is to achieve the indoctrination and submission of the Amazonian peoples through evangelization to allow the entry of transnational oil companies such as Shell itself. The indigenous organizations of Ecuador remember the SIL as one of the most disastrous chapters in terms of the loss of their cultures, languages, and territories. They played a crucial role in achieving the oil interests of the Ecuadorian State and foreign oil companies' objectives.

FLW: Historically, oil companies have divided the local indigenous tribes to fracture indigenous social movements. It's been reported that petroleum interests have armed and paid pro-drilling indigenous groups—and are suspected (allegedly) of aiding in violent attacks and the murders of indigenous anti-drilling advocates. Do you have any first-hand knowledge of this?

DFT: The role of oil companies, public or private, national or foreign, in breaking the social fabric of Amazonian indigenous communities is undeniable. There is too much academic literature on that. However, it is challenging to have first-hand information about these events because they are hidden even with the participation of the State itself. For example, in 2013, one of the most regrettable recent events of violence against Amazonian peoples occurred, the massacre of the Tagaeri resulting from an attack by the Waorani people of Dicaro. Thirty (30) Tagaeri people were exterminated. It is speculated that it was the oil companies that handed over firearms to carry out this massacre. This case is being resolved in the Inter-American Court of Human Rights.

Another more recent example is that of Eduardo Mendúa, Cofán leader of the A'i Cofán community of Dureno, who was a leader of territories of the same CONAIE and who was murdered in February of this year (2023). Eduardo was one of the main leaders in the fight against oil exploitation in the territories of his community and the communities of the Amazon in general, and it is speculated that the order to assassinate him came from the state oil companies when they identified him as an obstacle. But, in both cases, it is very difficult to have first-hand information.

FLW: Former President Rafael Correa, during his tenure, launched an initiative to keep the oil in the ground. Why did he change his position and attempt to legalize drilling if it was in the Constitution to make it illegal to mine in protected lands?

DFT: The official version is that it is because the initiative failed. In an exercise of co-responsibility, countries from the Global North failed to support the prevention of Block 43 exploitation, which was contingent on their contribution of 3 billion dollars. Not receiving the monetary support, there was no other option but to exploit the oil from this block within the Yasuni National Park.

Unofficially, it is known that Correa's intention was never to prevent exploitation, which was his campaign commitment and part of the political agreements that led him to the presidency for the first time. Exploiting this oil was always planned for him, but it had to be done in a way that would cost him politically, neither in votes nor in alliances. Some journalistic investigations have been published online about this.

FLW: Shortly after the courts ruled that the signatures on the referendum were valid, President Guillermo Lasso triggered snap elections. He dissolved the National Assembly before he could be impeached. How did the August 20th election affect the Yasuni Block 43 referendum? Did it help or hurt?

DFT: In my personal opinion, I consider that this political and electoral scenario did affect the vote in favor of Yasuní. Even in terms of the campaign, we had to campaign in favor of 'yes' during a very complex situation that relegated our Popular Consultation to the background. People were more concerned about the crisis we were going through at that time than about Yasuní, but we obtained a resounding result that left no room for doubt.

FLW: How did the referendum leaders operate between or around the left and conservatives on the right vested in oil drilling?

DFT: With certain exceptions, Ecuador's social and electoral left is aligned with positions in favor of the defense of Nature and against extractivism. Environmentalism is identified as a left-wing position. Therefore, these leftist sectors supported and campaigned in favor of Yasuní. On the contrary, the right-wing sectors demonstrated against Yasuní on purely economic arguments.

This reality has its nuances, more complex, of course, such as the positioning of the prominent leaders of the

Citizen Revolution, the political party of former president Rafael Correa, which announces itself as a left-wing party and belongs to the line of the Latin American progressivisms, which had a strong connection with extractivism, but with greater state control and use. But, even though Correa publicly rejected Yasuní, many of the bases and militants of the Citizen Revolution voted in favor of Yasuní.

Another similar case is that of the current president of Ecuador, who belongs to a classic Ecuadorian right-wing line, closely linked to the powers and economic elites of Ecuador, but who, during the campaign, publicly expressed his support for Yasuní. In short, they are very complex realities.

FLW: Given the unrest in Ecuador with a Presidential candidate assassinated, a sitting President implicated in associating with drug cartels, a pending run-off election between a leftist and a corporate conservative, and the fact that both political parties in the election serving the interests of major oil and mining interests it's a miracle that voters approved the referendum. How will the referendum remain intact with all the forces opposing it?

DFT: I always say that defending and ensuring the results are respected is as vital as winning the Popular Consultation. Without a doubt, that is our great challenge and primary obligation at this moment, and for that, we practically remain as if we were in an electoral campaign. One of our main strategies is the international visibility of this outstanding achievement to generate international pressure on the government and thus strengthen the results. Another strategy, of course, is social mobilization in the face of any attempt to fail to comply with the consultation results.

FLW: The election results were historic. Does the vote mean that the oil has to *stay in the ground* in the Yasuni National Park?

DFT: Without a doubt. Our Constitution and laws establish that the results of a Popular Consultation are *binding and mandatory* for the State and any other actor. Based on the decision of the Constitutional Court of Ecuador that approved the Yasuní Popular Consultation, within one year from the official publication of the results of the Consultation, the State of Ecuador must stop all oil exploitation of Block 43, remove oil infrastructure and ecologically restore the affected ecosystems and socially restore the affected communities.

FLW: Tell me who organized the communities and campaigns led by young Ecuadorian and Indigenous activists. How long did organizing different groups and building an environmental social movement take?

DFT: It was a potent synergy of wills. Many sectors were activated from their locations and with their resources to campaign for Yasuní. Many other people who have fought for the defense of Yasuní from the beginning also became active in their capacities. An essential moment in the campaign was the holding of the "Yes to Yasuní" Assembly, which brought together almost all the operational sectors and actors for Yasuní.

It was held in Cuenca and coordinated by Yasunidxs, the organization I belong to. In this assembly, actions were planned and coordinated at the national level for the campaign for Yasuní. On the other hand, it also coordinated with the CONAIE, which mobilized its bases and campaigned for Yasuní, specifically with the NAWE, the organization of the Waorani Nationality of Ecuador, whose members carried out a powerful campaign throughout Ecuador. Yasuní achieved a great mobilization of consciences and hearts.

FLW: *The vote changed the course of history for climate politics.* The public should be aware of the global impact. The legal precedent is that there's a limit to resource extraction. Correct? You must be so proud of winning in court and the election. What's next for you?

DFT: I agree. *The Yasuní Consultation set a global precedent in the fight against fossil fuels—an example to replicate worldwide.* And yes, the precedent is that citizens can limit the extraction of resources beyond the will of governments and companies. I am very proud to be part of these collective processes where many wills and efforts make it possible to achieve these achievements; nothing is achieved individually; everything is always collaborative. There are no heroes or messiahs. It continues to contribute to my abilities and responsibilities in these processes of struggle for Nature and the people, for life itself. More immediately, defend the results of the Popular Consultation of Yasuní against oil in the Amazon and the results of the Popular Consultation of Cuenca, my city, against mining in the paramos, ecosystems where the water we consume is born. In the same way, I will continue contributing to all the processes of defense of territories, biodiversity, and ecosystems of which I am a part; *that is my mission in life.*

FLW: It's safe to say that the oil and mining industries aren't going away. And environmental and indigenous activists will have to continue battling them in court and elections to preserve Indigenous rights, rainforest conservation, and global climate action. However, on the positive side, the Yasuni victory demonstrates that people can build social movements to protect biodiversity and the environment against the corporate and State power structures.

DFT: The fight we are fighting now is not only to stop these extractive activities but to transform the world and move towards new paradigms where human societies can develop without sacrificing the rest of the beings with whom we share the planet or offer life. It is a struggle to overcome capitalist modernity that is anthropocentric, ethnocentric, patriarchal, and classist. The great objective is to overcome this current stage and move towards a new world system. Understand that we are one in Nature and the cosmos; therefore, we must care for ourselves.

FLW: Social movements take money. *Where can people contribute to Ecuadorian and Indigenous legal environmental and social movement organizations?*

DFT: Indeed, social organizations need funds to sustain our activities. One of the most critical forms of support at the international level is the transfer of resources from the global north to the global south. In the case of Yasunidxs, we are not an NGO, so we do not receive resources from the State or other NGOs, so we do not receive any funds to carry out our activities. However, we do them. If someone would like to support us somehow, we should have direct contact to organize ourselves with that support.

The reason why Yasunidos is not an NGO is due to a security strategy to prevent the government from wanting to close the organization or affect us in any way through administrative processes.

FLW: I am familiar with *Nemonte Nenguimo, the Waorani indigenous leader.* Can you provide the names of other indigenous leaders and environmental activists who should be credited with the Yasuni referendum victory?

DFT: Of course:

- Alicia Cawiya, como lidereza Waorani.
- Norma Nenquimo, como Vicepresidenta de la NAWE.
- Juan Bay, como presidente de la NAWE.
- Leonidas Iza, como presidente de la CONAIE.
- Helena Gualinga, como vocera del colectivo Jóvenes Amazónicos.
- Pedro Bermeo, Antonela Calle, Sofía Torres, Fernando Muñoz, Alejandra Santillana, Manuel Bayón, Jorge Espinoza, como integrantes de Yasunidos en Quito.
- Esperanza Martínez, como representante de Acción Ecológica.
- Ramiro Ávila Santamaría, como abogado de Yasunidxs.
- Alberto Acosta, economista y académico.
- Emilio Chong y Xavier Viteri, como voceros de Resiste Yasuní.
- Fernando Bastías, como vocero de la Coordinadora de organizaciones sociales del Guayas.
- Klever Calle, Nidia Solíz, Paola Ortiz, como integrantes de Yasunidos en Cuenca.
- There could be more.

Photo credit, David Fajardo

FLW: In a world where State and corporate giants choose profit over people and the planet—the Yasuni referendum victory and Ecuador chose—Mother Earth. Would you agree?

DFT: I very much agree. In Ecuador, despite the economic crisis and oil being one of the primary resources for the State, citizens chose Yasuní, biodiversity, the life of indigenous peoples, and the Amazon over economic reasons to continue exploiting oil. In Ecuador, there is no greater democratic consensus than protecting Nature and caring for life.

All donations and organizational contact inquiries can be directed to David Fajardo Torres, Yasunidos Social Organization. Email: guapondeligyasunidos@gmail.com. WhatsApp: +593 987075453

YUSANI ANTI-MINING ADDENDUM
ORGANIZATIONS AND HUMAN RIGHTS ADVOCATES

Photos and descriptions provided by David Fajardo.

Photo credit, David Fajardo

This photo is of women from Ingapirca at the famous Canari/Inca Ingapirca archaeological site in Ecuador in the province of Cañar. David Fajardo worked on the project to create the Ñukanchik Allpamamanta Warmikuna Association, which in Spanish would be the Women for Our Land Association.

Photo credit, David Fajardo

My preferred means of transportation necessary on the Andean routes to travel to different communities.

Photo credit, David Fajardo

Photo of a pambamesa shared with the women of Ingapirca. In the Ecuadorian highlands, a pambamesa is a communal meal of food laid directly on a cloth spread on the ground.

Photo credit, David Fajardo

Photograph with the Coordination Group of the Community Water Government of Azuay, which brings together social organizations, water boards, irrigation systems, water channels, communities, and communes of the province of Azuay to generate social governance over water in the province. The photo was taken after holding a meeting with the province's governor on the issue of metal mining.

Photo credit, David Fajardo

The ancestral Andean opening ceremony of the "Meeting of Organizations and Communities of the South." It's where the National Anti-Mining Front of Ecuador was born, and we participate as organizers from Yasunido Cuenca. The event occurred in the Ancestral Commune of Zhina territories in the Ona Canton, Azuay.

Photo credit, David Fajardo

Photograph of the Rotary International Club awards event that recognized young people from Cuenca for their outstanding participation in various community areas. In my case (far left in photo), for environmental leadership.

Photo credit, David Fajardo

We were photographing a gathering of boys and girls from the Kichwa Commune of Llanchama, situated within the boundaries of Yasuní National Park. This Commune has successfully barred oil companies from accessing its lands, and we actively back their community tourism initiative.

A photo captures a gathering of the "Yawi" and "Warintza" Shuar communities, where the topic of mining in their lands was deliberated, with the Canadian mining firm Solaris Resources in attendance.

Photo credit, David Fajardo

Image of the traditional Andean ritual marking the commencement of Carnival festivities within the ancestral community of San Felipe de Molleturo, situated in the Azuay province.

Photo credit, David Fajardo

Photograph featuring the members of the Community Assembly of San Cristóbal in Galapagos, dedicated to safe-guarding Punta Carola Beach against potential threats posed by the construction of a large hotel complex, which could adversely impact the local species and ecosystems.

Photo credit, David Fajardo

(opposite) Photograph Captured at the General Assembly of the Shuar Arutam People During the Election of the New Government Council. This poignant photograph was taken during the Shuar Arutam People General Assembly, held to elect the new Government Council. The image showcases several notable individuals who have been instrumental in defending their territories against transnational mining companies and advocating for indigenous rights.

In the foreground, we find Josefina Tunki, the former president of the Shuar Arutam People, in a blue dress. She is widely recognized for her unwavering commitment to safeguarding her community's lands and resources. To the left of Josefina, we see Nathaly Yépez, adorned in black attire, representing the NGO Amazon Watch. She stands alongside her colleague, Raphael Hoetmer, who happens to be the tallest figure in the frame.

Moving further into the composition, we encounter President Tania Laurini and her trusted advisor, Tarquino Cajamarca, positioned behind her. Tarquino Cajamarca is a legal advisor to the Shuar Arutam People, lending invaluable expertise to their cause. The photograph also captures the presence of other Shuar individuals, who are members of the indigenous guard of the Shuar Arutam People. Together, they form a formidable collective dedicated to preserving their cultural heritage and protecting their ancestral territories. This evocative snapshot was taken after Josefina's tenure as the president, during which she played a pivotal role as a legal advocate against criminalization and served as an advisor on matters about collective rights and territorial defense.

Photo credit, David Fajardo

Capturing an image beneath a towering Ceibo tree in the Kichwa Commune's territory, known as Llanchama. In the company of individuals from Germany who were participants in a community tourism excursion jointly arranged with the Llanchama Commune to explore the wonders of Yasuni.

Photo credit, David Fajardo

Capturing the Essence of the Río Blanco Community: Collaborating with Acclaimed Filmmaker Marcos Colón on a Documentary Highlighting Women's Struggles, Indigenous Resilience, and Social Group Experiences in Ecuador's Paramos.

CARLOS LARA'S STORY
ECUADOR'S EMISSARY—SOUL OF A NATURALIST

"We need to find God, and he cannot be found in noise and restlessness. God is the friend of silence. See how nature—trees, flowers, grass—grows in silence; see the stars, the moon, and the sun, how they move in silence. We need silence to be able to touch souls.
—Mother Teresa

The picturesque city of Cuenca lies in the heart of Ecuador, nestled amidst the Andean highlands. With its winding cobblestone streets and stunning architecture, this UNESCO World Heritage Site has enchanted countless visitors. Yet, the charm of Cuenca lies not only in its architectural grandeur but also in its people. One name stands out as a true ambassador of Ecuador's rich culture and natural diversity: nationally licensed tour guide *Carlos Lara*.

Carlos is no ordinary tour guide. Erudite and charming, he's well-versed in his homeland's history, culture, and traditions. His knowledge is fortified by his personal and client experiences, anecdotes, and reflections. Conversations with Carlos are never one-sided lectures;

Photo Credit, Carlos Lara

they are interactive and engaging dialogues that are enlightening and inspiring.

One of the most striking aspects of Carlos's character is his demeanor; his ability to cultivate a sense of calmness and peace, even amid bustling city streets or rugged wilderness. It is this calmness that makes every tour an immersive and enriching experience.

A world traveler and bilingual, he effortlessly bridges language barriers and connects with people from diverse backgrounds. He's a maestro weaving captivating stories of Cuenca and the surrounding regions. Armed with decades of experience, he threads together tales of Ecuador's past and present, intertwining them with the tapestry of its landscape.

Carlos is more than just a guide. He's an educator and an embodiment of Ecuadorian charm and hospitality. He seamlessly weaves the Ecuadorian landscape's natural, historical, and spiritual elements, providing guests with a holistic understanding of the region. Carlos instills in his guests a profound appreciation for the delicate balance of the ecosystem and the importance of conservation.

A devout spiritualist, Carlos draws strength from his deep-seated faith; his spirituality shapes his interactions with nature and people. He sees heaven on earth in the cloud forests, the Andean valleys' rivers, and the Andes Mountains looming over the horizon. This spiritual connection to nature makes him a naturalist par excellence. His environmental knowledge is academic, spiritual, personal, and enriching.

He symbolizes what Ecuador represents—a fusion of rich history, diverse ecology, and warm hospitality.

Photo credit, Carlos Lara

He is a testament to the fact that the true essence of a place lies not just in its landmarks but also in its people. With every tour he conducts, every story he shares, and every question answered, Carlos is not just showcasing the beauty of Cuenca; he is sharing the soul of Ecuador. Referred to as Cuenca, Ecuador's emissary, Carlos embodies the spirit of his nation. His reputation extends far beyond the boundaries of Cuenca, earning him the respect and admiration of fellow Ecuadorians and international visitors alike.

Carlos has become a highly respected figure in Ecuadorian tourism with his vast knowledge, warm personality, and ability to connect with people. His dedication to his work and promoting his country's natural and cul-

Photo credit, Frederico Wilson

tural heritage has earned him the title of Ecuador's emissary. Through his tours, Carlos shares the magic of Ecuador with the world, inspiring his guests to appreciate and protect its natural wonders and historical treasures. In a world increasingly needing connection and understanding, Carlos's work is a testament to the power of shared experiences and the human desire to explore and preserve our planet's wonders.

CARLOS LARA
INTERVIEW

The interview with Carlos Lara took place at "Jodaco's Belgian Bistro" in San Sebastian Plaza, Cuenca, Ecuador, where both English and Spanish were spoken. Mary Wilson, a researcher and contributor, and Leonardo Duran, a translator, participated in the interview. The text has been reconstructed and edited to augment consistency and clarity.

[Abbreviations: CL: Carlos Lara, FW: Frederico Wilson, MW: Mary Wilson, LD: Leonardo Duran.]

FW: Carlos, thank you for joining us. We first became interested in interviewing you after we viewed your contributions to the 'Go Explore Ecuador' videos on YouTube. They were professionally produced and highly informative. We had the good fortune of meeting Lori Zabroski a principal part of the team that created the videos. As founder and editor of the Escaping Culture book series, I tell untold, unheard stories with origins in Latin America. That's an imprecise term describing South America, Central America, Mexico, and the Caribbean.

Nevertheless, I intend to foster and share authentic Ecuadorian perspectives, a larger frame of reference for others worldwide to consider and contemplate. So that's where we're coming from, and we invite you to share your culture, family background, memories, hopes, desires, and feelings about your Ecuadorian life. In essence, we want to know how Ecuadorian culture has shaped you.

CL: Well, that's a big question. Let me start by saying that my parents are from here. My grandparents are from around the area, and my great-grandparents are from different places. Some are from Spain and England.

MW: I'm sorry for interrupting. Your English is flawless. Did you learn English in Ecuador or elsewhere?

CL: You know, I've been to several places because of the studies I pursued. I went to England, Spain, and finally, the U.S. Because of my language skills, I've had the opportunity to visit Uruguay, Colombia, and several other places. I participated in a cultural exchange program in England when I was nineteen. I volunteered at a school for disabled children. While there, I stayed with the family of one of the girls from the school.

FW: Very commendable! Where in England did you visit? I'm sure you experienced cultural nuances there.

CL: I visited Shelton. A family whose name escapes me was situated not far from the area I explored. What struck me during my visit was the remarkable consistency in their behavior and interactions. Whether it was the parents or the children, their mannerisms remained remarkably uniform.

You would think that because England is so far away from Ecuador, people would think and act differently, but in the end, I found people in England, especially in that particular area, think similarly.

Later, when I returned from England, I focused solely on studying. Initially, I aspired to become an engineer or an architect. However, my path shifted when I stumbled upon an advertisement in the newspaper for a travel agency seeking English speakers for seasonal positions. Intrigued, I applied and unexpectedly found myself deeply immersed in tourism. It quickly became apparent that this was my true passion, and I embraced it.

After training as a tour guide, I discovered my passion for agency work. It was what I truly enjoyed, and I became known for it. Meeting people and honing my skills further solidified my desire for this career path. Additionally, I seized the opportunity to improve my language skills, mastering English through practice and immersion during trips.

FW: You speak French as well?

CL: I used to speak some French. But it's been a while. Most of my clients are English-speaking, so I'm out of practice.

FW: That happened to my Spanish; you lose it if you don't use it.

CL: Upon my return from England, I perceived Ecuador through a new lens.

MW: Traveling will do that to you. It broadens one's perspectives and outlook on life.

CL: Later, I had the opportunity to save money and travel. So, I went to the US for a couple of weeks initially. Then, I went on an exploratory trip above and beyond that. There were good opportunities to stay there, pursue a different profession, or settle in the US. But at that point in my life, I had a relatively good profession here, along with friends and family.

FW: Where did you go in the US?

CL: I went to New York City, New Jersey, and then to Miami.

FW: (Light-heartedly) They could all be considered different countries.

CL: (Nodding, smiling) Yeah, sort of. I was very impressed the first time I visited the US, but after just 15 days, I gained much weight. It took me a month to readjust to my regular eating routine when I returned home, sticking to my usual foods. It made me realize that US food likely contains some additives.

MW: Without a doubt, virtually everything on store shelves in the US contains additives. We found that all the food here in Cuenca is locally grown, natural, and organic, making it significantly healthier.

CL: I love to travel and visit other places, but I would definitely choose to live here. That's where I feel at home. Also, I've continued exploring and working here, trying to discover more about our culture, making new friends, and gaining a deeper understanding of the people around me.

FW: Do you notice cultural distinctions among the people in Ecuador based on their geographic regions?

CL: The culture here in Cuenca is distinct from that of Quito, Guayaquil, or any other region. Each area has its unique characteristics. It's similar to the differences in the United States. For instance, as you mentioned, Miami has a distinct atmosphere and way of thinking. These differences are part of the rich tapestry of diversity we experience in Ecuador.

Let me give you an early Cuenca cultural distinction. Do you know the tall building in Parque de la Libertad? People go up there to get a view of the city, right?

ALL: Nodding, yes.

CL: That building was once a prison, but initially, it was a temperance home, a place designed to help individuals with alcohol-related issues. However, its role evolved over time. It transitioned into Cuenca's prison. Previously, the town's method of law enforcement was primitive; justice was often dispensed before the Church, symbolized by the "humiliation cross," where wrongdoers were publicly whipped before being banished. Residing in Cuenca demanded honesty and integrity. Theft was inexcusable, and people were expected to uphold virtuous conduct.

FW: Residing in Cuenca demanded honesty and integrity. I get it. Before we could reside here, we had to submit FBI reports, marriage licenses, bank records, birth certificates, and proof of income. We couldn't have a blemish on our records. Cuenca checked everything.

CL: I'll give you another example. Have you been to the Yungilla Valley?

MW: We have yet to go.

CL: It's a lush, warm valley with fruit trees, frequented by many Cuencanos who own weekend retreats there. It's a place I wholeheartedly recommend. My grandfather owned a parcel of land in that area and once mentioned his intention to sell it. Intrigued, I expressed my interest in purchasing it. However, he regretfully informed me that he couldn't sell it to me as he had already committed to another party. Reflecting on this, I realized the significance of his integrity and the importance of keeping one's word, even at personal cost.

In this community, honesty in business dealings is vital; agreements are upheld with firm commitment, and transactions are often sealed with a simple handshake. This attitude resonates deeply with me.

In addition to my involvement in real estate, I also buy and sell cars. One notable aspect of conducting business here in Cuenca is the adherence to agreements. However, while people are amiable in Guayaquil, there's a tendency to obscure pricing and tax details. Meanwhile, Quito has a sense of elitism and entitlement. Each region has distinct attitudes, accents, culinary traditions, climates, and approaches to life and business.

FW: Aside from safety concerns, honesty was a significant factor in our decision to come to Ecuador. While I had conducted business in Venezuela, Colombia, Brazil, Chile, and Argentina, Ecuador was uncharted territory for me. Through extensive reading and research, we concluded that Ecuador presented a more favorable environment for conducting business and residing here than other countries in the region. We've been pleasantly surprised.

CL: So, what you mentioned earlier about biography, biology, and geography—these are the fundamental elements of culture.

FW: I believe so. Biology and geography have greatly influenced you. You're a naturalist, right? As a tour guide, these interests have significantly impacted your life. That's what intrigued me about interviewing you.

CL: First and foremost, I am a people person who adores nature and thrives as a tour guide. Nature fascinates me, and I appreciate the opportunity to explore different places. Being a tour guide satisfies my passion and provides me with a fulfilling profession. Over twenty years in this field, I have never faced a challenge that diminished my enthusiasm for it.

FW: We understand that it took you three years to become a licensed and certified Ecuadorian tour guide.

CL: It was a unique three-year course. When you pursue your passion professionally, it's truly a blessing. Being able to earn a livelihood, especially in a country as diverse as Ecuador, is something I'm deeply grateful for.

FW: Tell us a little about the people using your services.

CL: People who typically visit have a genuine appreciation for nature's beauty and serenity. Our region boasts diverse natural wonders, including majestic mountain ranges, picturesque coastlines, lush forests teeming with wildlife, and the awe-inspiring Amazon rainforest. They go to the Galapagos, Peru, Colombia, Brazil, Uruguay, Chile, and Argentina from here. They are after beautiful experiences.

MW: Exactly. That's the way we looked at it. We decided to live in Cuenca, use it as our base, and travel throughout South America.

CL: And some people are older people who left their baggage behind. Their kids are grown. They're retired and financially independent.

FW: But you know I've noticed more and more young people in Cuenca. Many more remote workers and people are escaping the stress of America, Canada, and Europe.

CL: Yes, more and more. That's a good thing. Let me tell you about a visitor who could have been better. I conducted this tour paid by the Chamber of Commerce in Quito for an ex-President of Mexico, Vicente Fox.[1] He was here to give a talk.

FL: I remember him well. He was a piece of work.

CL: Rude. What a horrible person. He thought he was king of the world. After the tour, I studied his life and didn't find meaningful things to be proud of. The guy didn't care about my commentary, the people, or the city. Nonetheless, I remember his wife as a very friendly and lovely person.

On the other hand, I had a client from France, a representative from a wealthy ministry. Unlike Fox, he paid for the tour.

---

1. Vicente Fox Quesada, a Mexican businessman and right-wing neoliberal politician, served as the 62nd President of Mexico from 2000 to 2006. His tenure was marked by controversy, particularly in the highly disputed 2006 elections, which were widely criticized by neutral election observers as fraudulent. In those elections, the PAN candidate Felipe Calderón was declared the winner by a narrow margin over López Obrador.

All: (Laugh)

CL: He hired me for a few tours, and I found him quite extraordinary. Having previously visited Ecuador, he spoke excellent English. However, the most intriguing experience occurred when I took him to an indigenous art exhibit at a museum.

When conducting tours, I prefer to tailor the experience to the client's interests. During one tour, we visited a museum where my client, in particular, found immense joy, especially in the stone sculptures on exhibit. He was captivated by a piece crafted by an indigenous artist. He spent a good 20 minutes admiring it, expressing that it was the most beautiful thing he had ever seen. He then asked me to assist in locating the artist and obtaining contact information. After reaching out, I discovered that the sculpture was available for purchase, priced at $12,500. Upon relaying this information to the client, he promptly acquired it. Interestingly, he later mentioned that he would have been willing to pay $100,000 for it!

FW: Seriously? Amazing. The artist could have inquired about what the piece meant to the client. I can only speculate on the potential value in such a scenario.

CL: In this case, both parties were satisfied with the transaction. The client arranged for its shipment to France through a specialized company. He even shared a photograph of it proudly displayed in his home! The point this is the type of experience I've had with various individuals throughout my tours.

FW: Flipping the script, I'd like to get your impression, in general terms, of how most Cuencanos perceive European cultures. We know Europeans, especially from the Northern regions, have preconceived notions about South America shaped by media portrayals and historical and political narratives, not to mention limited personal interaction. Stereotypes influence their perceptions. Has it been your experience that people from Europe—the North—understand people from South America? Do Cuencanos understand people from different countries in Europe?

CL: Cuencanos may have deep knowledge of some European countries, but there's a curiosity and openness to learning about different cultures. Some even choose to stay here. We're sitting in a Belgium Bistro, yes? The owner married a local Cuencana and started the business by making Belgian beer from his home.

MW: Their relationship undoubtedly bridged cultural preconceptions and knocked down barriers.

FW: I can attest to that from personal experience.

CL: (Smiling, acknowledging Mary and my mixed marriage) I find Germans fascinating. West and East Germans are very different. East Germans are very friendly. Very humble, respectful, and eager to learn. I like Germans, very much. Very quiet. They are like this piece of paper, like this glass. They observe. They're there, that's it. *They don't get excited about anything.*

FW: But a clear distinction between East and West Germans?

CL: Definitely.

FW: Without getting too deep into the weeds, the Cold War, the Wall, and reunification have much to do with it. Their collective culture took a beating.

[Pause in the conversations as food and drink were brought to the table.][2]

CL: You know I once took a tour to the Quilotoa Loop hiking trails.[3]

I admire Andean flutes, which are incredibly easy to play. I tell people on the tour, "If you see anyone selling flutes in the village, I would love to talk to them." As we wandered the town, we encountered an Indigenous man selling them. We approached and asked him if we could interview him. He agreed. "I have a small hut where I store potatoes from my land," he explained. "We can meet there."

So before we parted, I saw this chicken, right? I asked him if the chicken was his. He nodded, and I wondered if we could buy the chicken from him. We're going to hike to Crater Lake, I tell him. While we're gone, "How about you cook the chicken with the potatoes you brought back from your land? We can pay you for the chicken, have lunch with you, and we can play our flutes. So, we hiked to Crater Lake, enjoyed the fantastic views of the lake, mountains, and sunset, and then returned. We went to his place, where the guy served a delicious chicken dish with potatoes and we played our flutes.

MW: What a unique experience. The convergence of cultures and traditions highlights every culture's richness and diversity.

FW: I traveled extensively throughout South America, and before relocating here, I always tried to familiarize myself with the geopolitical landscape of various countries. *I recently read "The Confessions of an Economic Hitman."* It offers insights into the United States' involvement in Latin American nations. The author explained in great detail how the CIA installed dictatorships and neoliberalism policies so US corporations could cheaply extract sovereign natural resources from virtually all South American countries. It was a fascinating expose on the last 75 years of Washington hegemony.

CL: I read the book. I am trying to remember who gave it to me, but I remember his references to Omar Torrijos of Panama in the sixties and Jaime Roldos Aguilera, our former President of Ecuador, in the late seventies.

FW: As you probably know, Torrijos defended Panama's right of self-rule and its claims to sovereignty over the Panama Canal. Jaime Roldos was at odds with the Reagan administration. They were both human rights advocates. And both died in plane crashes. Very suspicious. Anyway, I didn't mean to go off on a tangent.

So, Carlos, in all our meetings with interviewees, we ask them what makes their lives meaningful and fulfilling. The answers range from very personal to philosophical, from self-discovery to aspirational. What's your purpose in life, Carlos?

---

2. *At this point of the interview, Carlos recalled another tour experience. Unfortunately, I have misplaced my notes of Carlos's recount of the memorable experience. I've pieced together his narrative from memory, relying on our conversation as a reference.*
3. *The Quilotoa Loop hiking trail is one of Ecuador's most sought-after adventures. It winds through the breathtaking Ecuadorian highlands and link several rural farming villages. What truly sets the Quilotoa Loop apart is the awe-inspiring Crater Lake (Laguna Quilotoa), surrounded by majestic Andean volcanic peaks.*

CL: *My purpose in life is guided by my faith as a Jehovah's Witness. So, I've read and studied the Bible.*

FW: Faith. I was going to ask you later about what you put your faith in, but go ahead.

CL: I started studying the Bible with Jehovah's Witnesses about 25 years ago, but I began taking it seriously only 15 years ago. I've been deeply engaged in studying the Bible, understanding the prophecies, and delving into the mission of Jesus when he came to the world and the entire system. Trying to understand the world through that knowledge has really molded me. My purpose in life is to be a good servant to Jehovah and serve Jehovah God wholeheartedly.

FW: Spirituality is an integral component of culture. Alongside social interaction and language expression, spirituality is crucial to cultural identity. These elements, including the arts and sciences, collectively shape a society's cultural landscape. When discussing Ecuador, it's essential to recognize and address these fundamental cultural elements.

CL: That's enlightening to me. Understanding the Bible, you see life with different eyes, for instance. Now, I treasure the experiences in my life more. *I treasure people. I cherish my wife and my son. They're priceless.* I feel grounded. Good balance, right? That's my purpose in life in a few words.

MW: You're grounded spiritually and through your love of nature. That's a beautiful thing.

CL: I think so. What more can a person ask for? I've been very blessed. I have many more experiences and memories I could share with you, but unfortunately, I have another appointment this afternoon.

FW: Before you go, what do you want the world to know about Cuenca and Ecuador?

CL: I would like people to know that Ecuador is not only about the Galapagos, nor do corruption and Indigenous issues solely define it. There's more to it. I want people to recognize that places like Cuenca stand out as beautiful examples of nature and culture, reflecting the richness found in all countries.

Every country has breathtaking locales and incredible people, offering unforgettable experiences. Ecuador is one such place; if someone seeks a fulfilling life experience, they should consider visiting. That's the service I aim to provide to my clients—not just tours but immersive experiences that open up new perspectives.

FW: Thank you so much for sitting down and sharing some of your experiences and insights.

CL: It's been a pleasure.

Photo credit, Jeff Schinsky

CUENCA ARCHITECTURE
A NARRATIVE IN STONE

Cuenca is a city of immense architectural splendor. The passage of time is imbued in the cobbled streets and the stucco facades of historic buildings. Designated as a UNESCO World Heritage site in 1999, Cuenca is a feast of architectural styles, representing the entire gamut of the city's layered history. The city's surroundings are an eclectic fusion of pre-Colombian, Canari, Incan, Spanish colonial, French, and contemporary influences.

From its early beginnings as a Canari settlement, transformed into an Incan stronghold, and eventually transforming into a Spanish colonial city, Cuenca has emerged as a beautiful mosaic where the threads of indigenous, Incan, and Spanish cultures are intricately woven into the fabric of the city's architectural landscape. Each period has left an indelible mark, etching its identity onto the city's edifices, streets, and squares.

The city's heart is the historic district, brimming with artistic gems from the colonial era. Cathedrals, churches, monasteries, and homes showcase the grandeur of Spanish colonial designs, where white-washed facades harmoniously meet red-tiled roofs, evoking nostalgic elegance.

In the canvas of Cuenca's architecture, every brick and tile, every arch and dome, *tells a story*. They speak of ancient civilizations, conquests and colonization, culture, artistry, faith, fortitude, and survival. Yet, they also speak of a city that continues to evolve, hosting and embodying *stories within stories* in its historic heart.

Cuenca is an architectural spectacle—a narrative in stone—where history and modernism meet, engage, and create something magical.

The city's Spanish colonial architecture is perhaps its most defining feature, characterized by a harmonious array of ironwork balconies and intricately carved doors. These historic structures, mainly influenced by Moorish, Andalusian, and French designs, are a testament to the city's rich past and influences. Noteworthy among them is the imposing Catedral de la Immaculad Concepcion or 'New Cathedral,' a grandiose expression of the Old World's Baroque inspirations, its Romanesque and Gothic blue domes piercing the skyline.

Cuenca also embraces the new, integrating modern architectural elements into its historical past. Contemporary high-rise buildings, museums, and art galleries co-exist with the old, connecting the past and present.

Cuenca is not merely a city where architecture is observed; it is a city where architecture is experienced. Its buildings and public spaces are a testament to human aspirations and accomplishments, forming a rich architectural story narrating the city's past while embracing its present and future.

THE CARLOS ALBERTO IGLESIAS CABRERA COLLECTION

Photo Credit, Carlos Alberto Iglesias Cabrera

HOTEL EL VADO, CALLE LA CONDAMINE

INTERIOR OF THE CHURCH OF SANTO
DOMINGO (INTERIOR DE LA IGLESIA DE
SANTO DOMINGO)

GATEWAY TO THE CATHEDRAL OF THE IMMACULATE
CONCEPTION (PUERTA A LA CATEDRAL DE LA
INMACULADA CONCEPCIÓN)

CHAPEL OF THE MARIANITAS ON BENIGNO MALO AND SANGURIMA STREETS (CAPILLA DE LAS MARIANITAS EN LAS CALLES BENIGNO MALO Y SANGURIMA)

THE JUDICIAL COURT BUILDING OF AZUAY ON SUCRE AND LUIS CORDERRO STREET (EDIFICIO DEL TRIBUNAL JUDICIAL DEL AZUAY EN LAS CALLES SUCRE Y LUIS CORDERRO)

SIDE DOOR OF THE CHURCH OF SAN ALFONSO (PUERTA LATERAL DE LA IGLESIA DE SAN ALFONSO)

BROKEN BRIDGE (PUENTE ROTO)

ESCALINATA DEL HOTEL CRESPO

INTERIOR OF THE OLD SAN LUIS SEMINARY
(INTERIOR DEL ANTIGUO SEMINARIO SAN LUIS)

REAR BUILDING OF THE MANSION ALCAZAR
HOTEL, LOCATED ON SUCRE AND TARQUI
STREET (EDIFICIO TRASERO DEL HOTEL
MANSION ALCAZAR, UBICADO EN LA CALLE
SUCRE Y TARQUI)

WINDOWS OF THE CATHEDRAL OF THE IMMACULATE
CONCEPTION OVERLOOKING THE CALDERON PARK
(VENTANAS DE LA CATEDRAL DE LA INMACULADA
CONSEPCION CON VISTA AL PARQUE CALDERON)

NOCHE DE CORPUS CHRISTI

COLEGIO BENIGNO MALO

BARRANCO DEL RIO TOMEBAMBA

GATE OF THE MUNICIPALITY OF CUENCA ON BOLIVAR AND BORRERO STREET (PORTON DEL MUNICIPIO DE CUENCA EN LA CALLE BOLIVAR Y BORRERO)

OLD SAN LUIS SEMINAR AND THE CATHEDRAL OF THE IMMACULATE CONCEPTION, BENIGNO MALO AND BOLIVAR STREET (ANTIGUO SEMINARIO SAN LUIS Y LA CATEDRAL DE LA INMACULADA CONCEPCION, CALLE BENIGNO MALO Y BOLIVAR)

BOLIVAR CLINIC, BOLIVAR STREET AND JUAN MONTALVO (CLÍNICA BOLÍVAR, CALLE BOLÍVAR Y JUAN MONTALVO)

PUENTE MARIANO MORENO SOBRE EL RIO
TOMEBAMBA

FRENCH BUILDINGS LOCATED ON BOLIVAR AND
BENIGNO MALO STREETS (EDIFICIOS FRANCESES
UBICADOS EN LAS CALLES BOLÍVAR Y BENIGNO MALO)

LEONARDO DURAN'S STORY

LITTLE BIG MAN

How do you measure a person's worth? It's not determined by their accomplishments in life but rather by the challenges they conquer.

[Abbreviations: LD: Leonardo Duran, FW: Frederico Wilson]

When one delves into the heart of the human experience, we occasionally encounter tales of perseverance, resilience, and triumph against the odds. These stories resonate across the bounds of culture and time, universally captivating our collective imagination.

Two seemingly disparate characters who embody these qualities are *Leonardo Duran,* a tenacious young Ecuadorian, and Jack Crabb, the protagonist of Arthur Penn's 1970 American Western film "Little Big Man," played by Dustin Hoffman.

The first striking similarity between Leonardo and Jack is their modest origins, which, despite their distinct ethnic, racial, and cultural backgrounds, provide them with a shared narrative of humble beginnings. Leonardo, a compassionate young man and small in stature from an indigenous community, has known the burdens of pov-

Photo credit, Leonardo Duran

erty, systemic discrimination, and educational barriers. In parallel, Jack is a Caucasian child raised in a Cheyenne tribe in the wild American frontier, an outsider navigating the complexities of Native American culture. Leonardo and Jack embraced multicultural identities, proving adept at reconciling diverse perspectives and using them to their advantage.

Their societies marked both Leonardo and Jack as unlikely to succeed. The hardship, however, bred resilience in them. It made them perceive life as a mosaic of learning, growing, and adapting opportunities. Both developed a spirit and weathered adversity, yet they were not beaten or cowed. These shared experiences molded them into the men they later became, shaping their worldviews, informing their decisions, and igniting a fire of ambition.

Their narratives further converge as they move toward their entrepreneurial ventures. For Leonardo, this began with the seed of an idea and the dream of leveraging his roots to build a sustainable business in Cuenca. He saw opportunities where others saw limitations, a quintessential entrepreneurial perspective. Jack, too, transformed his outsider status into an asset by leveraging his unique perspectives and experiences within his adoptive tribe to navigate the white-dominated frontier's business world.

To be sure, their journey to success could have been more linear and smoother. They faced formidable obstacles, resisted societal constraints, and overcame countless setbacks. The barriers were primarily systemic for Leonardo, rooted in socio-economic conditions and cultural marginalization. In Jack's case, the challenges were essentially societal, deriving from the prejudices and cultural misunderstandings of the time.

Leonardo and Jack succeeded through tenacity, resilience, and creative problem-solving despite the odds. Leonardo's success was defined by his ability to build a successful business grounded in his Cuenca roots, turning perceived disadvantages into unique selling points. Jack's success lay in his ability to straddle two worlds, utilizing his diverse experiences to build an enterprise in the ruthless world of the American frontier. Both Leonardo and Jack are testaments to the indomitable spirit of the underdog. Their narratives underline the transformative power of perseverance, and the triumph serves as a reminder that one's origins do not dictate one's destiny.

The stories of Leonardo and Jack, as unique as they are, show the universality of the human spirit. They remind us that the human story is one of resilience, adaptability, and enduring belief in the potential of change across continents, cultures, time, and circumstances. Their stories serve as a beacon of hope, a testament to the fact that, while formidable, adversity is never insurmountable.

The size of one's heart and the strength of one's spirit ultimately define the path of one's life.

LEONARDO DURAN

INTERVIEW

Leonardo Duran's interview was conducted at La Cigale Restaurant, Cuenca, Ecuador. This conversation has been edited and condensed for clarity. The commentary was added for context and perspective and to bridge the discussion.

[Abbreviations: LD: Leonardo Duran, FW: Frederico Wilson]

FW: So let's begin. Leonardo, you were recommended to us by a host of people as the tech guru here in Cuenca, and my wife Mary and I arranged a meeting with you at the Grand Colombia Hotel.

LD: Yes, correct.

FW: You told us a little about yourself during the initial meeting. I told Mary we had to interview this young man at the time because he's got a hell of a story to tell.

LD: Nodding.

FW: Think of this meeting as an extension of our previous conversations. Let's get comfortable and order some wine.

LD: Sure.

Photo credit, Leonardo Duran

99

FW: Introduce yourself. Where were you born and raised? Your age? Occupation?

LD: My name is Caesar. Well, Cesar Leonardo Duran Ramon. I was born here, in Cuenca, at the local hospital, but I grew up in Baños, a little town outside of Cuenca. It's about 15-20 minutes from where we are right now. I'm 39 years old.

FW: Everybody in this town, including expats,[1] seems to know you.

LD: (Laughing) Yes, before doing tech support, I worked for the Xerox Company and Apple through a local distributor, making sales related to graphics, arts, and various printing and outsourcing services.

FW: So you were born here. Where did you learn English?

LD: I was kicked out of my house at about 13. I then made my way to the States. I learned English there. I grew up in the States.

FW: Thirteen? You were still a child. Tell us a little about your childhood before you went to the States.

LD: Oh, I thought I was a pretty normal kid. I played around with other people and kids around my town. But I was very hyper. My Mom couldn't handle me. That's the reason, like I said, I got kicked out. My Dad had already left the family and gone to the States. Back in the 90s, Ecuador was a mess with politics and money.

FW: You were on the Sucre.

LD: That was the currency. Sure. And inflation. So everything was expensive. People didn't have money, and people didn't really have a way to survive. A lot of people went to the States illegally. My Mom started to see how well they were doing. They would get dollars and send them back home, and you could get a lot of stuff.

FW: How did your Dad get there?

LD: He has yet to tell us the actual story.

FW: What?

LD: One day, he told us he was in New York.

FW: (Shaking my head) Okay.

LD: I knew he had to pay a coyote[2] to get there. Everybody knew that the coyote worked two blocks from a local market and was a legitimate business. So you would go to the back of the store, and hundreds of people would be waiting there, begging coyotes to take them to the States.

Back then, I was still going to school and a kid going out with friends. I was never into drinking or smoking, but my older friends were—so my Mom assumed I was going that way, right?

I would tell her I didn't drink or smoke. She didn't believe me because I would—escape from home. I would go out the window. I would wait until she fell asleep, take off, and then return at six in the morning. She thought I was waking up and would tell me to do something. I'll be like, sure, Mom. I was a rebel.

After a while, my Mom couldn't deal with it anymore. So she said you should go to the States with your Dad. But back then, I didn't want to go to the States. Back then, I was really into music and especially liked English

---

1. *People living outside their native country.*
2. *Colloquially, a coyote is a person who smuggles immigrants across the Mexico-U.S. border.*

music. So, I would listen to cassettes and be amazed by the lyrics. So that's what I used to learn English.

About a block from my house, this lady had a store, like a bazaar, that sold all kinds of little things, including cassettes and CDs. My Mom, God bless her. My Mom bought me a bunch of these cassettes. She got credit for three months, and she would pay a little every week for the cassettes.

FW: Like layaway?

LD: Yeah, she would pay every week. I don't know how long it took her. Three months. My Mom was always helpful that way. Anyway, I would collect cassettes and CDs. Back then, I would listen to heavy metal and hang posters on the walls. My Mom thought I was worshipping devil music (laughing). That's about the time I would leave home for days at a time. I'd take off.

FW: How did your family take you leaving?

LD: My sister was more mature than me. She used to tell me that Mom was very upset with me and suffering. She'd say, "You've got to put your shit together, man—don't do that kind of stuff to Mom. She really cares about you." But I had an attitude, and I didn't care. So we would argue and fight, and I didn't want to do anything. That's when she just gave up on me.

One time, I went to Quito with four of my older friends. On the way to Quito, we crashed the car. We left it in the middle of nowhere and took a bus to Quito to the San Francisco Plaza. We stayed in a little hotel and fooled around for two weeks until we ran out of money.

Of course, we saw reality quickly. My friend Adrian and I needed money to pay for the hotel. So I have family in Quito, and I go to them thinking that's a good idea. Of course, they called my Mom, and that's how they discovered I lived in Quito. That's when my Mom made the decision. I will send you to your Dad to work in the States. So, I left to live with my Dad in Westchester County, New York.

FW: You went from Cuenca to Westchester County? How did you get there?

LD: So my Mom got brainwashed by this coyote guy, and the same guy took my Dad. So he told my Mom I would fly from Quito or Guayaquil to Mexico. And then, from Mexico, I would take a bus to the border, walk half an hour, and be in the States. *Welcome to the magic (sardonically).* Welcome to the American dream, right? That trip changed my life. I left here in the first week of December and arrived in the last week of March.

FW: How old were you again?

LD: 13.

FW: Thirteen years old and on your own? Tell me about the trip.

LD: Yeah. So, this coyote was the leader of the pack. There were about 80 of us. We went to Guayaquil. We stayed there for a few days waiting for the plane, right? They put us in cars and took us to the beach. And we're like, "What are we doing here?" So they got this big boat. And they're like, "Okay, get on the boat. You see the light over there? That's where we're going to go." And everybody is in shock at this point. "Hey, you told us we were going to a plane."

So this guy kept chilling on us and said, "Well, if you don't want to go, that's okay. But you lose your down payment." Three grand. So everybody just got on the boat, and then we're off. So we followed and got to the light—it was a fishing boat. They put all of us into the boat next to the engine and took off. You know, that's how I lost part of my hearing because I was right next to the engine for eight days and nights. I don't know if you've ever been at sea for a long time; you get very sick.

So anyway, we're maybe four or five hours offshore, and we hear gunshots! So we're like, oh, *we're screwed.* We thought we got caught by the police, right? No, it was pirates!

FW: Pirates?! Where were you?

LD: We had no idea—we couldn't see anything. We see a mass of water, right? That's it. It was night. They stripped us down to our underwear. Everything. Even females, everything. They took everything: underwear, shoes, clothes, everything. They put it in a bag. I remember them saying to me, "Give me the money." They hit me with a gun (pointing to his head). I got a scar right here in front of my head.

FW: So you were pistol-whipped?

LD: They took everything. It lasted the whole night, and they even took the engine! So we were in the middle of nowhere with nothing and had to turn around and go back.

FW: How did you get back?

LD: Another boat found us and towed us back to Guayaquil.

FW: So, what happened when you got back to Guayaquil? What did the authorities do?

LD: Nothing. Nobody said anything. We just went back to the hotel. We showered and wanted to know if the coyote would try again. He didn't want to because of what the pirates did to him. You see, they got everybody naked, and they wanted to know who the coyote was.

After finding out, they got two of their biggest guys with machetes and hit the coyote, buck-naked on the bottom until he gave up all the money. It was painful to watch. A machete against his butt. Unbelievable.

So anyway, we went back to Cuenca. I tell my Mom that there's no plane. Man, this is how they do it. So my Mom and everybody went back to the coyote in Cuenca. He says, "If you want to cancel everything, okay. We won't take your kid. That's okay. But you lose the deposit." So, the same thing happens: you lose the deposit.

FW: How did this guy stay in business or, for that matter, stay alive? Seriously.

LD: People were desperate to leave, man.

FW: I thought there would have been some blowback. So you escape with your life, and you return to Cuenca. And on top of all that, did you lose 3,000 bucks?

LD: Yeah. The situation could have been more favorable for all of us. But you have to do it that way and have no choice. Another week later, I left again, like before, to the same boat. You have to understand there's a network in place. A lot of people were going back then. A chain of coyotes was getting a lot of money from people, investing in businesses and drugs. They had big companies. So the Government sees what these guys are doing.

FW: Yeah, I can see why.

LD: Yeah, yeah. So, the Government changed the requirements for leaving the country.

FW: From what I understand, 50 to 60,000 people leave annually.

LD: Right. It just changed two years ago. The Mexican Government stopped allowing Ecuadorians to go into Mexico without a visa. They saw that most people were using Mexico as a way to the States, and they shut it down.

FW: So you go again . . . to the same boat?

LD: Yeah, so we get to Guayaquil. I go to the boat. I'm shitting my pants because what if this happens again, you know. What happens if the thieves show up again and we get robbed? Funny what you remember. This time we ate—chicken. I remember it was delicious. We get going. The second night, we got hit by a storm, and I'm curious if you've ever been in a storm.[3] It is the worst thing. It lasted the whole night. We lost everything we were carrying for eight days for the trip. The next day, we woke up, hoping for something to eat, and there was nothing.

LD: So we must stick it out for seven days without food. *Jesus.* Yeah, just water. Thank God it rained. They had a big tank, and that's what we drank. The only thing that I could find to eat was rotten bananas and lemons on top of the boat. That's all I ate for six days. See my front teeth? They're fake; they fell. The skin on my face was filled with blisters because of the sun and the seawater. It was just awful. We go for about seven, maybe eight days. There was nothing but water and sky. So we finally got to Guatemala. I was such a kid. We land, and I can't stand

---

3. *FW: Storm-at-sea experience—Dory fishing off the Oregon Coast; The Oregon Resurrection essay excerpt—Book: Escaping Culture—Finding Your Place in the World*

Oblivious to both risk and ridicule, we trudged on. And on this one inauspicious occasion, we also confronted darkness, a dead engine, and a short-circuiting radio that spat out intermittent blips, much like the crackle of a dying fire. We knew that every dory in the fleet was equipped with a radio. We were sure that somebody would eventually hear our distress calls. "Slick Willie (name of our boat), here," Rich would shout into the mike. "Can anybody hear us?" Nobody did. Uh-oh.

The fog engulfed our boat. We lost sight of the coast. The waves rolled higher; a horizontal rain was battering us senseless. Not even Kentucky Bourbon Whiskey could insulate us from uncertainty. We put on a brave face but knew we were in deep trouble. Woozy with the irony of having been born and reared in the desert and in imminent danger of being flushed down an oceanic urinal—I did what came naturally when confronted with the sudden turn of events. I took several more swigs, lifted my face into the pelting wind and rain, and shouted—to nobody in particular.

"Are you fucking serious?!"

Drenched, exhausted, and humbled, I remained glued to the mast until providence intervened. Between static transmissions and the pounding waves against and over our bow, another dory made radio contact and found our abducted boat drifting out to sea with its searchlights piercing the darkness. They tethered a line to our dory and slowly towed us closer to shore. With our engine now stammering to life, our rescuers released us so we could attempt to ride the surf to the beach. You see, dories don't dock. To get to shore, they must perfectly time and hitch a ride on the crests of waves. In inclement weather and in the dead of night, it's all a crapshoot.

So there we were, getting our bearings, navigating Haystack Rock, a massive mountain of granite a mile offshore, waiting for our engine to kick in. The radio was now buzzing with the fleet of fishermen on the shore, and they turned their truck headlights out to sea to guide us onto the beach. We made one last circle around the rock, grabbed the boat mast, and Rich put the pedal down on Slick Willie.

By this time, we were laughing hysterically. I guess that's what you do when you're scared shitless but don't want to show it. We hit wave after wave, and with each new breaker cresting early, we nearly swamped the boat. Undaunted, we gunned the engine until we finally caught a big swell just right and mercifully rode it safely to shore. From then on, Slick Willie was immortalized and served as comic relief to the Pacific City Dory fleet. But we didn't mind. Hell, we went fishing again the next day in the same damn boat.

up. At this point, I almost died a bunch of times, and I was laughing because we managed to get to Guatemala.

I want to remember the name of the city or the place. We started walking, and we walked through the mud the whole night. I remember the mud being up here (motioning to his waist).

So we get to this house. That was the first time I ever tried tortillas. *I hated those things.* (I winced, being of Mexican descent). I was like, what is this? I saw the lady making them in front of me. Tortillas and black beans. I didn't eat them for a few days, but that's all they ate. Hey, Guatemala, right? So we stayed there for 15 days.

Then they moved us to another house. And I got stung by bees, and *I'm allergic to bees.* I almost died there because there was no medication. So they gave me alcohol and cigarettes to smoke. That's how they tried to get rid of the allergic reaction. It seemed like that's all they did: drink alcohol and smoke cigarettes. So I think, okay, this is the way it is. Then we moved to another house.

FW: To another safe house?

LD: Yes. Exactly. We slept on the floor. The worst thing about this trip is not knowing what will happen next. The coyotes don't tell you when you're leaving, you know? You could be there one day, or you could be there for a month. You never know.

So we were in that house when somebody started yelling, "Let's go, let's go, let's go!" So we get up, about 80 of us, and they walk us into a field to a truck with a big pipe. You know those pipes where you put the gas? There were benches inside the pipe. So everybody sat down like riding a horse in front of each other.

FW: Damn, inside a pipe? Let me stop you there. I used to be in the heavy equipment and hydraulic business. Around 2001-2002, I was in Venezuela, and one of my clients who had been kidnapped and held for ransom showed me a *pipe* he used to escape his kidnappers. We stopped the car on the side of a muddy country road outside Caracas next to a donkey pulling a cart filled with junk. My client pointed across a field to a building where he was held hostage and to an adjoining sewer pipe he crawled through to escape. Some serious shit was going down in Venezuela at the time.

Someone without experience in Latin American countries would have been shocked. But hey, back in the day, most Latin America was messed up. Mostly gangs and imperialistic, IMF, and CIA shit. Anyway, I've seen a lot of crazy stuff. Crooked multinational companies, military and Government operations in Sao Paulo, Brazil and Santiago, Chile; machine gun toting guards stationed in front of my Bogota, Colombia hotel; torture chambers in underground police stations outside Hermosillo, Mexico—so *pipes* serving as hiding places, escape routes, and coyote stations don't surprise me. The pipe reference brings back a lot of memories. Anyway, sorry for interrupting you.

LD: No, no, that's okay. I get it, man. So there's no airflow. They would open the hatch up sometimes so we could breathe. But every time there was a checkpoint, things got ugly. They would close everything up. The police would hammer the pipe to see if it was empty. At the first checkpoint, everybody stayed quiet. Nobody moved. Then we moved to a second checkpoint, then a third checkpoint, then the fourth one—*and we got caught.* I knew we were caught because we stayed there for almost two hours without air. People started to die. You begin to pass out. You don't feel much pain, everything becomes cloudy, and you get light-headed.

I remember the guy next to me hitting me, like, "Don't fall asleep." It got so hard that people got naked because it was so hot. The next thing I see, this police guy sticks his head inside the pipe. I think that's when I got up and saw bodies lying on the floor. The police asked for money, and you know it's called "La mordida." (The bite-bribe). We paid, they let us go, and we moved.

So we ended up in Puebla, Mexico. I remember clearly there was a volcano[4]—the one that's always fuming because it was right across from that, and you could see it, and it was in the middle of nowhere.

We went to this house, maybe some retreat because there was a pool and a place to play basketball. We stayed there for about two weeks. Same routine: we eat, we cook things.

FW: After what you've been through, did you ever consider staying there?

LD: No, no, no . . . my goal was to get to the States to see my Dad. This place was just a hideout. Then they moved us to another house. Same thing and the same business. We're there for a short time, and suddenly, we got to move again.

FW: So, how many are in your group at this time?

LD: I think about 80. We got into a trailer; hundreds of people were already there. *Everybody was standing up.*

FW: When you say trailer, do you mean semitrailer?

LD: A container trailer, and I could count more than a hundred people. The container was huge. And then, on the back of it, they put banana boxes. If the trailer door was opened, you could only see bananas.

Okay, we start moving. It was alright once we realized it was not just a couple of hours, but we had to stay in the trailer for days. Four-day trip. Standing up. No sleep. You can't sleep. You're standing up. There was a little rope that people could hold on to so they didn't fall asleep, and every time I tried to sleep, I would fall on top of some shit. That's painful. It was disgusting. So I went to the back of the trailer next to the boxes. I went there because I couldn't keep up anymore.

I slept there for the rest of the trip. The next thing I remember is that I'm opening the banana boxes. Everybody was so hungry that they destroyed those things. If anybody had opened the trailer door, they would have found us inside. Like there was nothing covering anything. They finally opened the trailer and told us we were in the Sonora desert.

FW: Damn . . . I was born and raised in the *Sonoran* desert.

LD: Oh, really? So you know we're in the northern part of Mexico. Everybody was exhausted, and everybody lay on the ground and fell asleep. I remember I had one blanket from the Puebla place and covered myself. The coyote came and gave us a warning. I remember him saying that if something happens, just run up that hill. So I, the two guys that came along, instantly fell asleep on the floor.

The next thing I know, I hear sirens. I ran as fast as possible and managed to get to that hill. I remember see-

---

4. *Popocatepetl is an active stratovolcano in the states of Puebla and Morelos in Central Mexico*

ing the ones who didn't run getting back in that trailer. Oh my God! But that could have been a good idea because that's when things got ugly: we got lost in the desert. We were lost for about four or five days. I don't remember the town we found, but we found everybody else who escaped.

You know coyotes only lead at night and never walk during the day. They hide you during the day. They have codes when they hide you. They put a bunch of branches on top of you. You try to sleep and don't move because the Migra[5] tries to trick you.

They start calling you, "Hey, let's go, let's go, let's go." Do you know what I mean? And then people come out, and that's what they get caught? So, the coyotes give us a code to avoid that. No code; stay wherever you are.

So the coyotes gave us the code, and we got up. Let's go. Boom. Continue. They gave us a little food: tuna and tortillas. That's all you ate. So you fall asleep and get up. Eat something and continue doing it.

After about eight days of walking in the desert, we reached a small border town. Super. Yeah, I remember them picking us up on the highway. We ran across the road, and everybody got into a van on top of each other. Bam. We go to an American Gringo house. I remember them having a bunch of people there. They're normal, just living life. Like, that was their thing. Do you know what I mean? It was their house with a bunch of immigrants in it. Yeah, a white American family just cooking and doing everyday things. Kids going to school and stuff like that.

FW: How many people are in your group?

LD: About 10 people, and the coyotes put the other 70 in different houses.

FW: So they handed you off to another safe house network?

LD: Yeah, and then again to another network. They're going to take us to Los Angeles. And the way they do it is they take two people, maybe three people, in fancy sports cars. I remember entering this nice Mitsubishi Lancer with a baby light in the trunk. It was one of those trunks that had a clear window. So I could see everything. Okay, because I'm little, they put me in the trunk. Actually, the trunk was comfortable. I remember going through Las Vegas because I saw the lights. Oh my God, I made it to the States, you know? *So happy!* So we continue and make it to LA.

FW: And to another network?

LD: Yeah. We had to pay all of those people that took care of us. *We now belong to them.* So we paid our coyotes. They then had to pay everybody who helped us with every leg of the trip. So, I stayed in an LA apartment for about a month. Most of the time, I sat alone in the corner watching "Blood In, Blood Out." And "Mission Impossible."

FW: "Blood In, Blood Out?" I've never seen that.

LD: It's a Mexican gang movie. I could be one of the actors in the film because I know it by heart. *I became Mexican because of that movie.* It was frustrating because I stayed there for a month. Most people hide for a day and get a piece of paper saying they're Mexican. You go to the LA airport with that paper and fly wherever you need.

---

5. *La Migra is a Spanish slang term and refers to U.S. Immigration Enforcement, i.e., ICE and the Border Patrol are both referred to as La Migra.*

FW: What paper was that?

LD: It was a little certificate, a birth certificate.

FW: Really?

LD: Yeah, no need for a passport back then. Just a little piece of paper that says what your name was. My name was Juan Salazar. I was Mexican and 21 years old. Nobody would believe I was 21 or even 18 if you could see me back then.

FW: (Laughing) You don't look 39 now.

LD: So I finally got to the airport. I was the happiest guy and didn't even know where I was going. So the guy with us told me I got to go that way.

FW: And where was that way?

LD: JFK. I remember we got there, and I'm thinking like an Ecuadorian. You get to a bus stop, and my Dad will be there, right? Uh, no. I'm screwed at this point. My Dad told me about LaGuardia Airport, so he'll wait for me there. Let's go. So we are going to LaGuardia with this cab driver, but this is a huge airport, and I am still waiting for someone to expect me. While driving, I remembered my Dad told me he lives in Portchester, New York. I remember him saying something about King Street or Regent Street. So I said we got to go to Portchester. My Dad lives in Regent Street. Let's go over there. We got into a yellow cab with no money. Nothing. The guy in LA gave us five dollars. That's all we got. So, we went to Port Chester, almost an hour from this airport.

Regent Street was about three miles long, and King Street seemed 20 miles long. It was, you know, a big city. The cab driver was so nice. I mean, he took us all over the place telling people he's got two guys that were lost at the airport, and do you know them?

FW: Do you remember his name?

LD: No, man. He was an angel, for sure. This guy drove us around for hours.

FW: And he knows you can't pay him, right?

LD: Yeah, who does that? But after a while, he gave up on us. I'm thinking, "What do we do now?" I was with somebody else who was also going to Portchester, right? So we parked at a laundromat for a while. The cab driver needed to speak Spanish. We tried to communicate with him, but he didn't understand. He could have just kicked us out and left. But he continued to drive through streets in Portchester, asking people if they knew my Dad. Nobody knew him.

So we return to the laundromat, and a lady sticks her head into the cab. "Are you David's son?" And I'm like, "What?!" "They've been looking for you at the airport. Come with me," she says. So she paid the cab driver and took us to her house. I asked this lady, "How did you know it was us?" She said the cab. There are no yellow cabs in Portchester. There are only black cabs, and they're Cadillac-looking. The yellow cabs come from either the airport or the city.

And that's how I got into the States.

FW: But for the grace of God and a yellow cab?

LD: Yeah, that's when I started to live with my Dad. *But I went into culture shock.* I cried so much. I never got used to it. I only lived with him for a year. He worked at a roofing company. He used to drink and misbehave. I had to leave and live on my own.

FW: Where did you go?

LD: I went to see my cousin. He's like, my brother. He said, "Yeah, come live with me." He put me in a bit of space underneath the staircase. He put a little mattress in there, and people would throw stuff for the garbage truck to take on Thursdays. Some of it was good, and I found this big teddy bear. It was huge. So I was a kid, you know. I got to take this teddy bear with me. So he was my companion in my younger years. *He was my good news for years.*

FW: I understand; you were still a child.

LD: Yeah, yeah. I was a kid. So I had to get a job.[6]

LD: I got a job in construction. It was winter. My God! I was freezing! One day, I decided to take the train and go as far as possible. I would go to every restaurant and ask for a job. That's the only thing I could say in English.

So I go to a town nearby—Harrison, New York. I stop at different places and say I'm looking for a job. "Go away, kid," they would say. Nobody would take me seriously. They say, "You're not even 18, come on." So the last place I get to is this pizzeria called Pizza 2000. The name of the guy was John. He's from the States, but he's from an Italian family. He looks at me and laughs. He's like, "Are you kidding me? You're not 18. You're not even 15. Are you like 12?" I tell him I'm 18. He says, "What are you doing here?"

"I'm looking for a job," I tell him. I remember the delivery guys. They are all laughing and making fun of me. "Look at this little guy." So, John said, "I like you. You got balls, kid. I'm going to give you a job." So he gave me a job in dishwashing, and that's how I started in the restaurant business and *finished paying my coyote debt.*

FW: Tell me how you paid for it. How was that arranged?

LD: I owed $15,000. I would send money back to my Mom every week, every month. I would send every penny. I ate at the restaurant, and I kept the tips. That's when I learned about tips. I would clean the tables, and people would leave money on the tables. Should I take it? Should I ask the guys? *Like, there's money here.*

They're like, "Yeah, it's for you." Really? My God. So that was money for me. I learned other things. I learned how to do pastry. I used to do salads. So I knew little by little. That's how I paid the 15 grand that I owed.[7]

The last time I remember sending money, I said you know what? Now I'm going to go back to school. I knew I needed to learn the language, right? Because I will only stay for a year or two or something like that. I'm 17, approaching 18. So I said I had to return to school and quit the restaurant. I didn't even collect my last paycheck. I never went back.

FW: Do you ever think about that place?

---

6. *Early childhood job—Mexicans with Money essay excerpt—Book: Escaping Culture- Finding Your Place in the World:*

As a family, we were accustomed to manual labor. When hard times demanded, we worked the fields, picking cotton to make extra money and meet ends. One of my earliest childhood memories is helping my sister Cecilia pull a heavy burlap bag filled with the day's collected work through the seemingly endless bone-dry rows of white-puffed stalks.

7. *According to the Ecuadorian Foreign Ministry, the number of Ecuadorians attempting to enter the U.S. without a visa is less than 20% of what it was in 2020. In 2020, the fee was $12,000. Today it is $21,000 to $23,000. The higher fees result from a 2021 requirement that Ecuadorians entering Mexico have a visitor visa. —Source: Cuenca Highlife, 10/03/2002*

LD: I always think about the owner of that place. Oh man, I always think about it. I always think about the people who helped me and wondered what they're doing. Friendly people, you know? Also, I think of people who screwed me too. I think about them all the time.

FW: So, where did you go to school?

LD: I walked into Portchester Middle/High School, and I'm like, hey, I want to go to school.

FW: You just walked into the school thinking you could start classes?

LD: Yeah, I walked into the reception office, and I'm like, hey, "I'm here to enroll myself." They laughed. "You need a guardian, someone to represent you," they tell me. I'm like, wait, what? They told me to bring my Mom or Dad to enroll me. So I go to my Dad. Could you do me a favor? Can you come to this school and sign papers and tell them you're my guardian. He's like, yeah, sure. So he goes, signs papers, and boom. The next day, I was in school.

FW: Where were you living?

LD: I was living under the stairs with my teddy bear. *Yeah, with my giant teddy bear.* I love them. I have a picture of myself sitting next to this huge teddy bear, and I remember sending that to my Mom. It's got to be somewhere.

So I went to school, and since I wasn't working, I needed to pay my rent and everything. I got a job cleaning offices. I did that after school. I would go to school from 8 until 3. Sleep a little bit and then go at six part-time. That's what I did until I made a friend who had a friend who was a chef. The chef saw how I worked with a knife and asked me where I learned to do that? At the pizzeria, I told him. He says, "You want to be a chef?" Sure. "I'll give you a chance as a pastry chef. I'll show you everything." So I worked at this place for about two years.

I made Crème Brule, flan, cheesecake, and chocolate cake, everything you can think of. But then it was too much work for too little money. I would see my friend who would work half the time as me, and he made twice as much as a busboy. Okay, so now I want to be a busboy. They were making more money than the kitchen. They paid me about $600 per week. And that's when I got on the floor—they called it. I was really good at it, too. Little by little, I worked in the restaurant business for about 15 years. Meanwhile, I was going to school, too.

FW: So, how was your English when you entered Middle School?

LD: It was crap. I didn't understand anything. I had to actually go to ESL classes.[8]

I had to do that because my English could have been better. Later, in New York, I took regular classes, and I needed to do that to take the Regions exam. Did you hear about that one? It's a New York University exam to see if you were smart enough to graduate and apply. So, the University of New York would give exams to 12th graders. I took it, and because I was more comfortable with my English, *I passed it and graduated.*

FW: Congratulations! Incredible. You're the real Horatio Alger story.

LD: What? Who?

---

8. *English as a Second Language (ESL) programs offer international students the chance to learn English or improve their English language skills.*

FW: It's an American bullshit myth—about how *only* white Americans achieve success alone—through self-reliance and hard work. You should be very, very proud of what you've accomplished. You're the exception, and I mean the things you had to overcome. Anyway, go on.

LD: I kept on making money in the labor and service industry. Meanwhile, I'm living with some of my partners.

FW: You remained in the area?

LD: Oh yeah. I lived with a Colombian girl illegally for about three years. So this is what I did. I went to Greenwich, Connecticut, because I like friendly big cities and it's beautiful there. The town had many wealthy people from hedge funds and investors from Wall Street. I started working at a Barcelona restaurant, and they treated me nicely.

FW: So you're working in the restaurant business again. How about school?

LD: I went to community college. They charged me $5,000 because I didn't have papers and wasn't a local resident. I paid for it and took technology classes. But I always worked and stayed in the service industry.

Then, Bush[9] came up with this Safe Neighborhoods Plan Bill. *That's when Latin Americans got attacked pretty severely.*

I was attacked all the time, but it even got worse. I'll tell you a little story about Bush. He came up with the Safe Neighborhood Bill, which said that anybody with some record would be kicked out of the country.

FW: Compassionate Conservative.

LD: Bush came up with that one, but the Obama administration kept doing it.[10]

In 2010 in Portchester, N.Y. I got pulled over by the police because my plate number was mistakenly given to the police by a friend's girlfriend who, in a dispute with my friend, believed *my car* belonged to him. I was charged nevertheless, and because I didn't have papers, the police called ICE.[11] I was put in a detention center for 11 months even though I was part of the Dreamers.[12] I did everything right. I paid my taxes. I graduated, but they didn't let me go.

FW: You fell through the cracks.

LD: I was sent to detention centers all over the States. I went to New York, and I got moved to New Jersey. Then back to New York. Then Philadelphia, and then to Texas. Then I went to New Mexico.

FW: Eventually, you were flown to Guayaquil?

LD: Yeah, with chains on my two hands and my feet.

FW: Tell me about the deportation process.

---

9. *Project Safe Neighborhoods Bill—Establishing a network of law enforcement and community initiatives targeting gun violence in large cities— President term, George W. Bush*

10. *George W. Bush Presidency 2001-2009; Barack Obama Presidency 2009-2017*

11. *The U.S. Immigration and Customs Enforcement (ICE) is a federal law enforcement agency under the U.S. Department of Homeland Security. ICE's mission is to protect the United States from cross-border crime and illegal immigration. —ICE Wikipedia*

12. *DACA enables certain people who came to the US as children and met several vital guidelines to request consideration for deferred action. The individual must have proof that they entered the United States before age 16 and must have continuously lived there for at least 5 years, have graduated from a United States high school or obtained a GED in the US, and demonstrated good moral character.*

LD: So you see a judge, right? The first thing you do is ask for a bond. Some people get a bond, but most people don't. Obviously, I didn't. It's all up to the judge. So they take you to a detention center, but it's a jail. I mean, there's no difference. I remember meeting this guy. This black guy in Philadelphia. Fascinating guy and very friendly, too. I talked to him. He asks me, "What are you in here for?" And I said immigration. He's like, "I can't believe these assholes." And he tells me he is in for manslaughter. He's doing 30 to Life, and they have me sharing a cell with this guy. But he was a very nice guy. He took care of me for a while. Same thing with these Dominican guys. They really took care of me. They fed me, and they taught me how to survive in jail.

Jail time was probably the worst thing that's ever happened to me. It's something I don't wish on my worst enemy. Being incarcerated was one of the worst things that I had to endure. That wasn't good for my state of mind. It changed my life completely. I used to be this very social guy, and I used to trust people.

I remember calling friends from jail, asking them to send me money. I used to lend them cash. One guy owed me $500. Can you send me some? I'm starving. Please! "Yeah, yeah, send me the information. I'll send it tomorrow," he said. I never got it. I used to cry. I lost faith in people. And I said, you know, that's it. I'm on my own. Do you know how I survived? I learned how to play poker. And I ate, what do you call those noodles, Ramen? One time, I won 50 Ramen soups. I used to eat those every single day. I chilled. I learned how to do origami and some magic tricks in jail.

One time, I got put in solitary for 30 days because I got into a fight. I used to have this friend. I think he was from Guatemala. He was betting against a black guy. I think he was from Jamaica. So the Jamaican looks at me and says, "What should I do? You think I should go all in?" I said, "Yeah, go all in. He's bluffing." So, the Guatemalan folds. And the guy from Jamaica wins! His friend gets upset, and we get into a fight. They put me into solitary for 30 days.

Thirty days, it's terrible, man. My God. The only thing they give you is the Bible. Yep. That's all they provide you, the Bible. I've read the Bible from Genesis to the Apocalypse cover to cover. Yeah, I've covered the whole thing. I read the entire thing—out of desperation. And you know what's funny? *There were no white people in the Bible.* They wrote it. They wrote it, right?

FW: Not exactly. Go on.

LD: I learned to be patient. I'm not religious. But that was the only thing I had. Solitary is crazy because that's where they put crazy people. You can't sleep because people are kicking the walls and doors. It's hard, man. I used to get a paper towel and toilet paper, make little balls, and put them into my ears to make less noise. It was crazy.

So the judge in my case says you can appeal your case and fight, but that will take another 14 months. *No, thank you. Just kick me out (of the country).* So they moved me to another state. In that place, they put people into little rooms with air conditioning below zero, keeping them there for days. It's torture, man.

They make millions of dollars out of the immigration system from people like myself. They get paid daily for each one of us. They get paid, what, $200 per person? I mean, it costs less to go to college than prison.

FW: It's intentional—a social-engineered ethnic cleansing money-making scheme. So they deported you, and they put you on a plane?

LD: Yeah, they put a US Marshal on the plane, and he's in charge of you. Like I said before, everybody is in chains in the airplane. I got to Guayaquil in March 2011.

FW: So you're back in Ecuador but with a *new skill, English.*

LD: Yes. But here's the thing. I'm in culture shock. I wanted to blend in. But I'm *very anxious.*[13] I couldn't function socially. It was horrible. I couldn't go to the mall. I couldn't do anything. So I tried to look for jobs. I couldn't do it. It wasn't good. *I fell into a depression.*

I didn't know what to do. Then, I met my ex-wife, Danielle, a US citizen. She's from the States. She's white, from New Mexico. She was an exchange student. She was doing research on returned migrants. So I told her my story. Anyway, we met. I met her through an ad on Gringo Tree. I see this student searching for migrant re-turnees for interviews. She's like, let's meet. We met at the Magnolia Café.

She told me to meet her there at 3:00 PM. I show up on time at 3 PM, and she's not there. So I have a glass of wine. At 3:20, I thought she was not going to

Photo credit, Leonardo Duran

show up. So I sent her a message, and she's like, "Oh my God, I'm so sorry. Give me 10 minutes."

(Emotionally) She shows up. Okay, (holding back tears) I may get sentimental here. It's hard. So she showed up and *actually looked at me and listened. That's why I fell in love with her.* I tell her my story, and she looks at me and says, "How are you even here—how did you survive?" We talked, and I asked her if she wanted to hang out. She said she didn't drink at interviews, but "I'll have a glass of wine with you because I think you are more." That's how we met.

Two years later, we got married in Guayaquil. She was perfect for me and very supportive. She got me out of that anxiety, the social stuff I couldn't deal with.

---

13. *People with anxiety disorders have intense, excessive, and persistent worry and fear about everyday situations. Often, anxiety disorders involve repeated episodes of sudden feelings of intense anxiety and fear or terror that reach a peak within minutes (panic attacks). These feelings of anxiety and panic interfere with daily activities, are difficult to control, are out of proportion to the actual danger, and can last a long time. You may avoid places or situations to prevent these feelings. Symptoms may start during childhood or the teen years and continue into adulthood.—Mayo Clinic, Patient Care and Health Information*

Before we got married, she went back to the States. We were just boyfriend and girlfriend. One day, I was at work and said, you know what, I'm returning to the States. I don't care what's going to happen. I know the consequences, right? I've been through it already, and I've done it already. I just wanted to be with her. So I told her that I wanted to be with her. I told her this would not work out if we lived in two different countries. She didn't want me to risk it. So what did I do? I just took off. I did it all over again. Big mistake.

FW: Coyotes?

LD: Different coyote. So this time a girl from Cuenca was with me, right? We went to Panama and then to Guatemala. We took buses, and we got lost in southern Mexico. We were trying to figure out how to continue. So, at this point, I go and find a train. Have you ever heard about *La Bestia*?[14]

FW: Yes. Migrants ride on top of the trains to get to the States.

LD: They call it *La Bestia* ('The Beast') because so many people riding on top of the train die and get hurt. Many people get hit by trees along the track and lose their arms and legs. That's how it is. So I met this guy. I think he was from Salvador or Guatemala. He was with a girl. He's like, "Hey, you guys are going north?" He tells us, "I know the route." This is one of the most dangerous things I've done. You get on top of a train, and there's nothing to hold on to. He told me, "Just look up, nothing else." You don't even sit up because trees or under-

Photo credit, Alamy—2x38TDG

passes can hit you. That's how people die. So every day we stop someplace. We chill and wait for another train. At this point, I had an iPhone and could take pictures. I have a bunch of photos from that trip.

FW: What year was that?

LD: 2011 or 2012? I have videos of people on top of that train. We're talking about 200 to 300 people trying to get on the train. So anyway, we're on the train at night, and I'm just listening to my music. I saw this guy sitting down, smoking a cigarette. Then I felt something like a hit. I am still determining where I got the strength. I grabbed him by the foot. He's hanging on, and three of us pull him up.

Anyways, the guy we saved takes me to Nuevo, Laredo. He says, "If you want to go to the border, I got to take you to this guy." *Oh my God, I've never seen someone*

---

14. La Bestia ("The Beast"), also known as El tren de la muerte ('The death train') and El tren de los desconocidos (The train of the unknowns"), refers to a freight train that starts its route in Chiapas state in Southern Mexico, near the border of Guatemala. —Wikipedia

as fat as this guy. He sits on the edge of a bed and can't breathe. Huge guy. *He pulls a gun out of his pocket.* He says, "How can I help you?" I tell him, "I want to cross the border." He said it would cost me $3,000. I told him I had to call my Mom to send the money.

The guy we saved was grateful and told me he would care for me until I crossed the border. He takes me to a house to hide for two weeks until we get the okay to go. They took us to the river, and we swam and walked for about three hours. *And then we got caught by La Migra.*

Okay, I already know how the system works. They asked me if I would like to apply for such and such, and I told them no. Please kick me out. In three days, I was back in Ecuador. And then I tried a second time. I got caught again. But you know it wasn't traumatic anymore. I mean, because they (immigration) were like, this is a joke, *"Oh, you're here again?"* So, at this point, a judge tells me, "If you try to come back again, you will be put in detention and a federal prison for two years." And I said that's it for me. I decided to work as hard as possible in Ecuador, make a living here, and make even more money

Photo credit, Leonardo Duran

than I can in the States. When I came back, I did not fit in. *It was tough for me to embrace my own culture.*[15]

FW: Understood. You were living in two worlds. The irony doesn't escape me.

LD: I remember coming back here in March 2013, and eight days later, I got a job in marketing and sales at Xerox and Apple. Then, I got into the technology part of it. I would go to technical support, hang out with them, and ask them to show me how to do things. I'm

---

15. Identity conflict—*Pocho, Going Rogue essay excerpt—Book: Escaping Culture –Finding Your Place in the World:*

For as long as I can remember, identity by choice or force has wrought conflict and contradictions. Who am I? What am I? Where did I come from? Where am I going? My surname implies I'm white, but my brown skin begs to differ. Am I Mexican? My Mother's family tree most certainly is, but my Father's Celtic, Euro-Iberian branch bears my Anglo surname.

Am I more culturally European than ethnically Latino? Am I a Native American, rooted to my beloved Yaqui Abuela? To which ethnic tribe do I belong? The truth is that I've teetered on the edge of dueling races and ethnicities all my life. My admission was accepted or denied for equally irrational cultural and color-coded reasons. My detractors accused me of acting too white, being too dark-skinned, and not being Yaqui enough. They ridiculed me for not speaking Spanish fluently, not being from the "barrio," for speaking "fancy" like a gabacho.

By many, I'm considered a Pocho—a half-breed, an Americanized Mexican who has lost his culture. I'm an exile in the land of my birth. So, after dealing with these socially engineered absurdities, I decided to go rogue.

really quick, and I learned really fast. When they were swamped, they would call and ask if I could help them. I said, "Hell yes!" I was bored with marketing and sales, and I got good at it, and after a while, I started to do my own thing.

FW: You became an entrepreneur. That took guts, young man. I've been there and done that. You have to have faith in yourself and your abilities.

FW: Let me switch the subject. What do you think about when I say *faith*? What do you place your trust in? What do you believe in?

LD: Oh, it's always been me. Do you know what I mean? I've been through so much. But I grew up in a very religious family. You know how Cuencanos are, very Catholic. My Mom, she's a fanatic. I grew up with a fear of God. Something will happen to you if you don't do this or that. I grew up with that resentment, so I stayed away. (Smiling) Okay, I do pray once in a while. But I keep it to myself. I'm the only one that gets me out of trouble. So, yeah, it's me. I'm most proud of myself. I've been through so much stuff. I've grown up alone, basically. Even with my ex-wife, I was alone because she would leave for months. Like I said, she wasn't from here. She didn't live here with me very long. She lives in New Mexico. We communicated by cell phone, text messages, and WhatsApp videos. So that was hard.

FW: So basically, you were straddling two cultures. You were raised in Ecuador and the United States. Your American (white) wife lived in Ecuador for a while. Eventually, she moved back to the United States to pursue her career. You couldn't migrate legally, and you damn near

died trying to join her several times. That's a heavy load to carry.

LD: (Reconciled) Uh huh.

FW: You have a unique experience in both worlds. So, what would you say to anyone about the *cultural differences* you experienced?

LD: Oh, that's a tricky question. Well, the cultures are very different. I will give you a quick example. Before I married my US wife, her Mother used to think we lived in the jungle and had leaves covering our private parts. She believed that all of Latin America was dangerous and you would get shot or kidnapped. When they actually came here for my wedding, they were impressed. They said, "Oh my God, this city, this culture." They were amazed at how clean the city was. They were surprised at how educated people were and compared Cuenca to Europe. They said, "This city looks like a little European city." They thought we lived in the jungle before.

We're advanced in a lot of things. I mean the architecture alone. It's phenomenal. Beautiful. Oh my God. I became a photographer in my free time because of the architecture I love. I go all around the city and take pictures.

FW: Agreed, it's one of the best things we love about Cuenca. Structures are the footprints of previous civilizations.

FW: Let me ask you about *purpose*? What's your purpose in life?

LD: (Hesitant) I want to help other people. So you've seen me with Patricia, right? Patricia is my assistant because I want to help her. She's just a kid. She reminded me of myself as a kid living in the States. Nobody would give me a job. She's from Venezuela, and she's an immigrant. She comes from good people, from a good family that had money. But the Government screwed them over. They had to flee. She's from a business-class, upper-class family in Venezuela.

But Cuenca needs to give outsiders opportunities. Nobody wants to provide you with a shot. She was a kid struggling. No food. Sick. No chance for anything. So, I teach her what I know: investments, cryptocurrencies, and Wall Street. We have weekly meetings about that. For the first time, I have money to help people so they can avoid making the same mistakes I did. Seven to nine years ago, that wasn't even possible. I feel proud when I see her trying to do what I do.

So, one of my clients needed help renovating their property. She had an idea to landscape the place, and she sold the whole picture to this guy and made it happen. And I was like, I'm so proud of you. She started saving because I saved. My ex-wife taught me about budging, saving money, statistics, and investing. So I teach all of that to her. She puts money away monthly in her savings account. So I like that stuff. That's my purpose. It makes me happy to see her succeed.

I used to travel a lot when I was with Xerox. So I used to go around the country closing deals, helping businesses, and things like that. That's when I met Patricia's Mom. I love food. That's one of my things. I went to this Venezuelan restaurant, and that's when I saw her. She was so interesting because she was into everything. That's how we became friends. Over time, we lost contact, but one day, I got a phone call from her. She says, "I'm living in Cuenca." I was like, Wow! She's been my friend since she introduced me to her daughter Patricia.

FW: Good for her. Good for you. She's very fortunate to have met you. You can always have a few friends.

FW: Flipping the script, tell me—what comes to mind when I say *fear*? What are you afraid of?

LD: Oh, man. Incarceration. Being stranded in the middle of the ocean, and I don't know. *Being alone.* That's the thing I've always been afraid of, and it's my biggest fear.

FW: After what you've been through, that's understandable. What makes you *happy*, Leonardo? What or who do you love?

LD: Food and wine. Unfortunately, when I turned 35, I started to get stomach issues. Now, I can only have a few things. I had to change my diet. What makes me happy? Good question. I don't know. You think what makes you happy would be the same things people from the North make them satisfied. You know, material stuff. But we're talking about culture. Priorities. *Friends and family make me happy.* For a long time, that's something I didn't have.

FW: Northerners have families, too.

LD: Yeah, yeah, but I lived in both places. It's different here. Expats always make a point about families in Cuenca, taking care of the older people, kids running around in the park, and stuff like that. It's always about family, you know. Every time I talk to an expat, that's the point they make. Even now, I still love going to my Mom's. My Mom is seventy-six years old, and I love going to her house. She's the happiest person. She's always whistling. It makes me so happy. When we talk, my Mom says, "I'm so proud of you; you're doing so much

Photo credit, Leonardo Duran

right now with your business. You're even doing more than what you did in the States."

"Yeah," I tell her. "But Mom, I got a lot of experience in the States and learned the language." Without the language, I wouldn't have met my ex-wife, and I wouldn't have learned everything I know right now. I would need to learn how to handle failure. People need to understand what failure does. It teaches you. Failure is a big slap in the face.

So when I returned, I couldn't understand my Mom and younger brother. He would drink every week and would get home wasted. He was a mess and 40 grand in debt—so immature. My Mom felt so bad for sending me to the States; she spoiled him. He was her 30-year-old baby. She would say, "Oh, poor thing come here." One day, I told her, "What are you doing to this kid? You know, a little tough love would help." Parents claim they don't have favorites, but they do. She says, "I wish he was like you." I'm sure, Mom, send him to the States. Let him live 20 years by himself. Let him spend months in jail. I think every Mom has favorites.[16] He's in the States now and turned his life around. He sent money home to his family and got out of debt.

FW: Oh, yeah. I've written about it at some length. Parents are a trip. Look, you're obviously a sensitive guy. Let me change the subject to something more pleasant. Tell me about tender moments in your life.

LD: (Pausing) In the big picture, when I married. My wife cried in front of me. We had a traditional Ecuadorian wedding. We got married in Guayaquil. It was an ordeal, by the way. It was different than just going to the civil registry and getting married. Actually, we had to do a bunch of things since she was away from here. We got a special visa. We had to interview in different rooms. Questions like, why are you marrying? It may be because she was a US citizen. Many Venezuelans, Colombians, and Peruvians come to Ecuador for shelter. They try to take advantage of the system. We had to interview ten times. Her family came over. We threw a big party. It was beautiful and one of the most tender moments in my life.

FW: Let me ask you a couple more things, and we'll wrap this up. Given that you deal with many foreigners, what's your general impression of them?

LD: Most are nice people; 99% are friendly. But I've also met some extremists. I learned to stay away from some subjects. I'm the type of guy that keeps an open mind about things. When I worked for big companies, I learned there are certain things you talk about, right? I've had to deal with a lot of North American people. Like I said, they are friendly people. *They are very generous people.* And most of the time, respectful. But they bring some baggage with them. I take them everywhere, to stores, to buy phones, stuff like that. Sometimes, they complain and say, "Why don't people here speak English?" Are you serious? That's basic. *You have to try to learn the language.*

FW: Language. The fundamental pillar of culture. To embrace another culture, you have to first escape your own.

LD: Exactly. Some people need to do that, and many only develop economic ideas.

FW: Economic refugees?

LD: Exactly. They can't take it in the States anymore. They come with the idea that people here have to change for them. It should be the other way around. But, like I said, I keep an open mind about things. It's hard for them to mix in. But others embrace it, like you said. They respect our culture. They love it, and they help people, you

---

16. *Favorite Child—Parents Behaving Badly essay excerpt—Book: Escaping Culture—Finding Your Place in the World:*

You're not your mother's favorite child—or maybe you are—but you already knew that, didn't you? Nothing in early life affects us as profoundly as our parents. They're our role models, and we learn to emulate them—sometimes, at our peril. They influence our relationships and shape the people that we become. Better that, as adults, we escape their grip and construct our narratives by deconstructing their narratives about us. Only then can we extricate ourselves from their chosen world and move on to living on our own.

know. For example, I have this guy who is my mentor. North American. He's from Texas.[17]

FW: Texas? Really? I'm surprised. No, I'm shocked somebody outside Austin, Texas, would help.

LD: I met this guy through my work. He's really a good friend. And like I said, I'm grateful for what I do because I meet some fantastic people. We meet once a week to talk about anything and everything. And being the guy I am, I started asking him questions, and he turned out to have a Ph.D. in economics. So, we talk a lot about investing.

FW: As I said, I'm shocked. Over the years, I've done a lot of business in Texas. There are no handshakes in Texas, bud. Get everything in writing. There's a common joke about their unofficial state motto. *"If you ain't cheating—you're ain't trying."* Just a friendly piece of advice. So what should North Americans know about Cuenca?

LD: Cuenca is a fantastic city. We're unique. We're different from the coast and Amazonia. The people from Quito and Guayaquil have different attitudes. Cuencanos are all part indigenous. We come from the Canari and Quechua that settled here, and then the Inca came.

And funny, everybody claims they are Spanish, and some, like my Mom, think they're not indigenous. My ex-wife and I once talked about this, and my Mom said she was European. So we just laughed. My ex-wife got my

Photo credit, Leonardo Duran

Mom a DNA test to prove she was indigenous. It's all about status and things like that.

FW: Unfortunately, that's true throughout Latin America.

Well, Leonardo, we can roll with this. I can't thank you enough for sitting down and telling your story.

LD: No, thank you. I really liked it. I got a little sentimental. Everybody has a story, right? That's what I like about your project.

---

17. *Personal Texas Experiences—No Handshakes in Texas essay excerpt—"Upon arriving, I was escorted into a waiting room adorned with everything Texas, bronze horse statues, tacky Dallas Cowboy paraphernalia on the walls, miniature commemorative Texas and American flags in one corner of the room—even a longhorn bull encrusted silver spittoon wedged between a coffee table and couch. WTF? I thought I'd entered a parallel universe. A counterfeit culture without context. When I walked into the waiting room, I knew what they were selling, and I wasn't buying. The heart of the matter is that sometimes you have to go through it to go beyond it—Texas, that is."*

Photo credit, Leonardo Duran

FW: Every story matters, Leonardo. *Everybody matters.* It's what connects us. Your determination, perseverance, and survival—not giving up in the face of setbacks—are inspirational. Your testimony has made my life irredeemably better.

*Postscript: Leonardo, ever the entrepreneur, recently attended a social media conference in Dubai, where he took a "flier" on another business opportunity.

It's not a stretch to say nothing will stop this young man from reaching his goals.

GUSTAVO & ROSANA'S STORY

A Symphony of Fire and Ice—A Paradox of Enduring Love.

Within the rich tapestry of life's characters, some defy the typical expectations of harmony, their compatibility a source of continual intrigue. Allow me to introduce you to **Gustavo Cordova Vintimilla and Rosana Montesinos Mora.** Two extraordinary people my wife, Mary, and I had the good fortune of meeting and spending time with while living in Cuenca.

Picture this: A husband's personality embodies a roaring fire, bursting with unbridled energy and spontaneity. It might appear overwhelming, but it perfectly complements his wife's calm demeanor. She is reflective, contemplative, and firmly rooted in pragmatism. Their relationship showcases the enchantment of duality, demonstrating that disparities can serve as bridges rather than barriers.

Gustavo, a striking white-haired force of nature fortified with entrepreneurial and occupational experience and knowledge in the medical, aeronautics, auto, and banking industries, is an imposing figure, exuding a robust and powerful presence. His piercing eyes con-

Photo credit, Frederico Wilson

vey wisdom and authority, while his broad shoulders and sturdy frame suggest a life of hard work, play, and determination. He speaks with a voice that commands attention, his words infused with the passion and zeal of a man who has seen and accomplished much in his life. Add to that his propensity for giving public theatrical

121

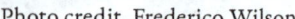
Photo credit, Frederico Wilson

performances of magic and mentalism—and his persona takes on added import and potency.

Rosana is equally impressive. Graceful and poised, she radiates composure—and is every bit Gustavo's equal in their relationship. As a matriarch, it's readily evident she's the calming influence and the cornerstone of their family, the stabilizing force in their relationship. Her love for Gustavo and her children is readily apparent, characterized by selflessness, sacrifice, and unconditional support.

As is their Ecuadorian custom, they welcomed us with warmth and kindness. They invited us to their beautiful ancestral country home, where we exchanged cultural, youthful, family, and children's stories and got to know each other personally. Rosana offered us her secret lasagna dish and traditional food servings: chulpi (corn with fava beans), mote, choclo (sweet corn tortillas), potatoes cooked in papa de sambo, and pumpkin seed aji sauce. Gustavo entertained us with magic: card tricks,

Photo credit, Frederico Wilson

bending forks, and disappearing coins. Our time with them only confirms that hospitality is a defining feature of Ecuadorian culture and a significant reason why so many visitors return year after year, and many choose to make Cuenca their home.

Their country home is a sanctuary, providing privacy and tranquility. The sounds of the river, birds singing, and the rustling of leaves in the wind creates a peaceful atmosphere, making it a perfect place to escape from the stresses of everyday life.

The house's interior features traditional design elements such as hand-carved wooden furnishings, brightly colored textiles, and intricate tilework. The rooms were spacious and airy, with large fireplaces and comfortable seating, creating a warm and inviting environment. It is truly a unique and magical property, offering serenity from the outside world.

Adjacent to the main house stands a historic mill house powered by a creek alongside the building traditionally used to grind grain, a living, breathing reminder of an ancestral past. Inside, massive wood beams support the thick adobe walls. Adorning every inch of the building are remnants, photographs of ancestors, paintings, firearms, pottery, a cache of denominational Sucre, and

Photo credit, Frederico Wilson

Photo credit, Frederico Wilson

Photo credit, Frederico Wilson

Photo credit, Frederico Wilson

Photo credit, Leonardo Duran

Photo credit, Leonardo Duran

tapestries—a museum of sorts, a tribute to who and what came before.

In relationships, a harmonious balance is often the foundation of enduring success. However, the captivating relationship between Gustavo and Rosana defies this common notion. Their bond is not a union of similarities. Still, rather a fusion of opposing elements—symbolized in their case as 'fire and ice.' Gustavo's impulsiveness and adventure personify uninhibited passion and intensity. He thrives on an innate fervor, engulfing all those around him in his boundless energy. This man does not merely exist in the world; he rekindles the flames of life.

On the other end of the spectrum, Rosana's ice—tranquil and composed embodies structure, providing a soothing comfort to the searing intensity of Gustavo's spirit and the fiery chaos around her. Resilient yet yield-ing, she embraces life's tumultuous events with serenity, providing a safe harbor amidst the storms of life.

So, how does this marriage of fire and ice endure? How can a relationship sustain such stark differences without melting the ice or extinguishing the fire? I suspect the secret lies in their understanding and acceptance of each other's distinctive energies. Gustavo's fiery demeanor is not designed to melt Rosana's icy composure, nor is Rosana's cool demeanor intended to extinguish Gustavo's passion. Instead, they serve as a balance for one another.

I imagine Gustavo's intensity on occasion drives Rosana beyond her comfort zone while at the same time encouraging her to embrace change and seek out experiences she would otherwise avoid. Concurrently, Rosana's tranquility tempers Gustavo's impulsivity, providing space

Photo credit, Rosana Montesinos Mora, Andrea Cordova Montesinos and Maria Fernanda Cordova Montesinos.

Daniel Cordova M.

for reflection. Their polar differences serve not as a wedge driving them apart but as a magnet pulling them together.

Their relationship is a testament to the beauty of diversity, illustrating that love is not a mirror that reflects similarities but a prism that celebrates differences. It's the way they understand and embrace each other's elemental nature—the way fire respects the cold restrain of the ice and the way ice admires the warm passion of the fire—which their love story unfolds.

The enduring relationship of this fire and ice couple is a heartening reminder of love's transformative power. Their bond echoes that compatibility is not rooted in sameness but in acknowledging and understanding our differences. Ironically, they have found a shared unity in their individuality, a paradoxical harmony that echoes in their enduring bond. This bond shows us the breathtaking beauty of a love story written in fire and ice.

In the world of science, fire and ice are depicted as opposing forces, elements that stand against each other. And yet, this metaphor of a marriage not only survives but flourishes in this dichotomy, where Gustavo is like fire, and Rosana, like ice. They've created a beautiful paradox, a unity that offers a rich and harmonious experience resulting in an enduring love story.

* * *

Gracias, Gustavo y Rosana, por recordarnos el hermoso viaje de la vida.
Cuando jóvenes tenemos un azar
caótico y apasionado
hambre de vida.
A medida que envejecemos, los apetitos de la vida
volverse refinado, culto y saboreado.
Esta etapa marinada de la vida
nos perdona que reflexionemos y aceptemos
nuestro tiempo aquí en la tierra.

* * *

Thank you, Gustavo and Rosana, for reminding us of life's beautiful journey.
When young, we have a random
chaotic and passionate
hunger for life.
As we grow older, life's appetites
become refined, cultured, and savored.
This marinated stage of life
pardons us to reflect and accept
our time here on earth.

GUSTAVO AND ROSANA
INTERVIEW

The Gustavo and Rosana interview was conducted in English and Spanish at Restaurante El Jardin inside Hotel Victoria on Calle Larga y Antonio Borrero, Cuenca, Ecuador. Mary Wilson, researcher and contributor and Leonardo Duran, translator joined us for dinner. The interview has been reconstructed from notes, audio text, translations, and recollections of conversations and edited to augment clarity.

[Abbreviations: FW: Frederico Wilson, MW: Mary Wilson, LD: Leonardo Duran, G: Gustavo, R: Rosana.]

FW: Thank you for sitting down for this interview.

LD: As you know, Fred speaks Spanish but not fluently. So feel free to converse in Spanish; if Fred doesn't understand, I'll translate your words. His latest book is about Cuenca, Ecuador's culture, and is called "Stories from the Andes."

FW: We want to know how Cuenca culture has shaped you. Feel free to talk about anything: your youth, how you met, and your passions, adventures, and misadventures. Let's say we begin. Tell us a little about yourselves.

G: We are retired. I hope our story isn't boring and centers mainly on our youth.

FW: Not to worry. I noticed that you used to perform magic in theaters in Cuenca.

Photo credit, Gustavo Cordova Vintimilla

129

MW: We've seen old posters of your act on Facebook and around town. How did you begin?

G: A captivating Spanish magician came to Cuenca as a young child. He left an unforgettable impression on me. I found myself fascinated by a world where reality mixed with fantasy. From that encounter, a curiosity for the mystical arts of illusion, hypnotism, and mentalism shaped my lifelong fascination with the mysterious and extraordinary.

FW: So, this childhood impression led you to performing. We should all deviate from reality to balance our outlook on life. From fantasy back to reality, what were your early and traditional job-related pursuits?

G: In my youth, I dreamed about becoming a doctor, healing, and compassion. That aspiration guided my academic endeavors, but fate steered me away to economics and commerce. It led me to trade and industry, where my professional pursuits became the art of negotiation and the science of markets.

FW: Life gets in the way sometimes. Invariably, it alters our dreams.

[Pause, wine being served]

FW: These are troubled times in Ecuador. Please tell us what you think about the indigenous strike.

G: The struggle with their organization persists among the indigenous community, a longstanding challenge. Despite some progress, familiar issues continue to loom in their path. Whether dealing with resource allocation, representation, or systemic barriers, they are locked in a recurrent cycle of old problems. They have to *adapt*

to the reality on the ground. On the other hand, their spirit fuels their determination to overcome obstacles.

FW: That's interesting and sadly prophetic. We're interviewing an environmental lawyer who is helping organize the referendum to stop the oil drilling in the Yasuni National Park.

R: That will be a fascinating interview.

FW: We're reading and seeing that they're better organized. Time will tell. We have cultures colliding.

G: A recollection comes to mind. As a young man returning from military school, I was uninterested in the structure of the Air Force. My father gave me crucial advice during this stage in my life: "Work, find your path." My father worked in a quarry then, and his friend, the tire shop manager, suggested I work there. And so, with humble beginnings, I entered the world of manual labor. It was here, with dust and sweat, that I learned the lesson of *adaptation,* embracing the challenges in front of me with determination.

FW: From there, did you go on to less labor-intensive endeavors?

G: Yes, of course. I previously mentioned I found myself immersed in the world of medicine. However, despite pursuing healing knowledge, I faced an unexpected obstacle. *Cadavers.* Despite the invaluable anatomical lessons they provide, they became an insurmountable barrier for me. They stifled my aspirations. Despite my best efforts, I realized that my path diverged from medical practice, leading me to seek alternative pursuits. (Ironically son, Daniel Cordova M. is a practicing physician).

FW: Cadavers? Who knew?

[All at the table: Laughter]

G: Yes, cadavers! Absurd, I know. Fate kept leading me down unconventional paths. I went from medicine to my ambition of becoming a pilot and found myself in another crazy situation. In training, my enthusiasm got the better of me. In a moment of thoughtlessness, I flew over the coast. I foolishly gave the beachgoers below an unexpected thrill, swooping my plane perilously low over their heads.

MW: Really? You buzzed a beach?

[Table roars with laughter]

G: My maneuver was ill-advised.

FW: You think?

G: People reported the event. Consequently, I was grounded. I was denied the opportunity to become a pilot. So, I once again had to *adapt* to fate. However, to this day, I'm amused by the incident.

R: Becoming a pilot was more than just a career choice for him; it was his deepest passion. It stirred exhilaration within him and fueled his dreams and aspirations. Who knows what would have happened to us if he had become a pilot?

FW: And how do you see your roles now?

G: We're now retired. I don't have any economic activity. We have a farm and spend time planting trees, flowers, and fruit for our grandchildren. We have two grandchildren. I am their "crazy grandfather."

R: Did you know he used to swallow swords and breathe fire? Whenever he sees someone on the street

Photo credit, Rosana Montesinos Mora

doing the same, he's always eager to snap a photo with his cell phone.

L: (Cringing in his seat)

G: Yes, I was 15 years old at the time. We were at the country house on the farm, surrounded by family and cousins—my father, mother, grandfather, and all our relatives. I had always been fascinated by magical stunts, and one of my favorites was practicing sword swallowing while it was ablaze. However, during one attempt, as I withdrew the sword from my throat, my face inadvertently caught fire.

MW: What!?

R: His grandfather brushed his face with a *wire brush for a year* until the burned skin was removed and the skin was healed and rejuvenated.

FW: With a wire brush? I was going to ask you if you have any regrets, but that takes the cake.

R: Regrets? The fire, of course.

FW: How about you, Rosana? Any regrets?

R: I would have liked to study more and had a career but I was already a mother.

MW: That's a career. There's no more important a career than motherhood.

G: For me, it was aviation and flying.

FW: (Shaking my head in disbelief). Excuse me, I can't get over your face catching on fire.

(Rosana nodded affirmatively, it happened.)

FW: (Still laughing) Ok, let's change the subject. Tell us what makes Cuenca unique?

R: Tell people in your book that people in Cuenca are good people. They are friendly, cordial, and affectionate with visitors.

G: Cuenca is like a bit of heaven. Tell them it's essential to meet and know people when they visit and live here. Our culture will tell them everything they need to learn.

FW: I will be sure to convey those sentiments in the book. We can't thank you enough for sitting down with us and sharing some of the moments in your life.

R: We would like to invite you to our country house to talk and show you more about Cuenca, our family and lifestyle.

MW: That's so kind. Just tell us when.

G: When will the book come out?

FW: We have a dozen more interviews, but we expect the book to be completed in late 2023 and published in early 2024. We're taking breaks to visit other countries in South America and Europe.

And with that, we can continue our conversations in our next meeting at your country home. Now let's finish our dinner and have some more wine.

DR. LORENA VINTIMILLA'S STORY
RISING ABOVE

A career of putting others before oneself for the common good.

t's early November, a typical summer evening in San Sebastian Plaza in Cuenca, Ecuador. My wife Mary and I have invited Dra. Lorena Vintimilla to Jodaco Belgian Bistro's outside patio to discuss her Ecuadorian story.

Uncommonly good-natured and personable, it didn't take long into our conversation for us to grasp her love for life and humanity and sense of belonging and station in life. What makes Lorena's story unique is how her personal fortitude, family support, and culture helped her rise above the biases endemic in the Ecuadorian male-dominated culture.

Lorena has transformed her life's adversities into a powerful journey of resilience and success, overcoming a gauntlet of childhood bullying and gender partialities that are deeply entrenched in Ecuadorian society. Her story is an inspiring testament to human will, fortitude, and the power of support from a loving and caring family.

As she tells it, Lorena's early years were shaped by the beauty of Cuenca and the richness of its culture. The

Photo credit, Dr. Lorena Vintimilla

133

Photo credit, Dr. Lorena Vintimilla

Photo credit, Dr. Lorena Vintimilla

landscapes filled her with love for life, animals, and nature, but her journey had its trials.

As an overweight young lady in a society where appearances often dictated self-worth, Lorena was frequently the subject of harsh bullying. These experiences could have stifled her spirit, but instead, they stirred in her a determination to rise above her peers' unkind words and misguided judgments.

Her parents, both professionals (Government and legal) who had broken their own barriers, instilled in her the understanding that her worth was not defined only by her physical attributes or the stereotypes surrounding her. They emphasized the importance of education and hard work, constantly reminding her that her intellect and kindness were her most potent strengths.

Lorena's grandmother, a woman of immeasurable wisdom and warmth, also played a pivotal role in her life. She constantly reminded Lorena of her potential and value, fostering a nurturing environment that taught her the beauty of humanity. Through the words of encouragement and moments spent with her, Lorena gained her passion for helping others.

However, navigating the path to becoming a physician in a male-dominated society was challenging. The biases and expectations placed on her as a woman were problematic, but Lorena's will remained unshakeable. Readily evident in our conversations, her innate good nature must have allowed her to connect with others, making her an effective communicator. No doubt, these qualities became vital as she struggled to make her voice heard in an environment that often overlooked women's potential.

Much to her credit, Lorena confronted her challenges with supreme confidence and perseverance—pushing against societal norms. Her innate empathy and intellect dispelled the notion that a woman's capabilities were less than a man's.

Remarkably candid, she willingly shared that her journey was not limited to her career. She tackled her weight issues with the determination that marked her educational and professional pursuits. She overcame this personal challenge with a healthier mindset toward her body image. Conscious of maintaining a balanced lifestyle, she didn't aim for an unrealistic ideal but worked toward achieving a healthier version of herself, acknowledging that the value of this transformation lay more in its impact on her well-being than any societal standards of beauty.

Attractive by any measure, Lorena is now an independent, highly successful physician, a shining example of hope and inspiration for many in her circle and beyond. Her journey of overcoming adversity demonstrates that personal or societal obstacles can be overcome through confidence, perseverance, and the unwavering belief in one's worth.

It would be remiss of me not to mention her unyielding and resolute dedication to patient care in Cuenca's hospitals during the Covid crisis. Imagine, if you can—being forced to make life-and-death decisions based on bed shortages, triage conditions, who gets admitted, and staff absences. Faced with those dire and calamitous realities, somebody less prepared and capable would have been crushed in the chaos.

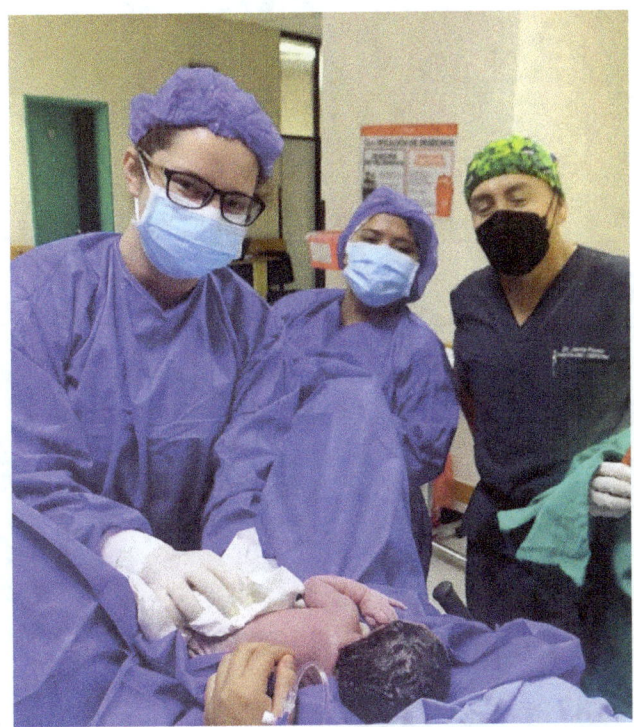

Photo credit, Dr. Lorena Vintimilla

I was happy to hear that she didn't dwell on the effects of the tragedies associated with the Covid pandemic and relayed to us how, as her time as an OBGYN physician, she maintained jars in which she puts little blue or pink balls representing the gender of the children, she's delivered.

Lorena's story is a testament to the transformative power of belief, an indomitable spirit, a family's love and support, and above all, understanding what can be achieved when one dares to dream big, work hard, and never let the constraints of society dictate one's potential.

DR. LORENA VINTIMILLA

INTERVIEW

Dra. Lorena Vintimilla's interview was conducted in English at "Jodaco's Belgian Bistro" in the San Sebastian Plaza, Cuenca, Ecuador. Mary Wilson, researcher and contributor, joined us for the interview. It's been edited for clarity.

[Abbreviations: LVM, Lorena Vintimilla Martinez; FLW, Frederico Lara Wilson; MEW, Mary Ellen Wilson]
[Seated at the outside patio, we see Dra. Lorena Vintimilla is approaching.]

FLW: Welcome.

LVM: [A gentle breeze blowing] It's nice to meet outside.

MEW: Good to see you again.

FLW: Given we briefly spoke earlier in the week, I assume we can skip the formalities. May we call you by your first name, Lorena?

LVM: Of course.

FLW: Thank you for responding to the invitation to meet. This is going to be less an interview than it is a conversation. We're anxious to hear your story. In front of you is a printout with a series of topics we'd like to cover. Let's relax and order some wine while you review the topics we'll cover.

MEW: I understand you just returned from attending to some patients in the States.

LVM: Yes, I got back on October 12th. My patients were demanding I come.

MEW: That's unusual. Traveling back and forth must be challenging.

LVM: My mother handles all my appointments. It makes it all possible.

MEW: Which airlines do you use?

LVM: American and Jet Blue. All others have layovers that are too long. I was in Massachusetts, Connecticut, New Jersey, and New York in October. It's an excellent time to go in October before it gets too cold. As a matter of fact, my Mom just talked with a friend in the region, and she told us that it's already getting cold.

MEW: It's so pretty here today.

LVM: It's magic. Much warmer. We may not have all four seasons—but in one day, you can feel the rain, the sun, cold, and warmth. Cuenca is magical that way.

LVM: You met my brother, Jose?

FLW: Your motorcycle riding doctor, brother? Yes, impressive young man.

LVM: I went to visit him in Guayaquil. He's doing his internship there. The weather doesn't bother him. He rides his motorcycle everywhere. He's happy there, learning a lot.

FLW: Doing his internship?

LVM: I told him that Guayaquil was his best option.

MEW: Why was that?

LVM: You know the city is not safe, right? [Nodding our heads.]

LVM: There are a lot of things that happen. It's

dangerous. People with knife and gun wounds go to the emergency room where he's working. So I told Jose (half-jokingly) you should go there because you'll get a lot of training. So, he went, and he's super happy.

FLW: He's young and living on adrenaline.

LVM: Yes, he had a 24-hour shift, and he tells me, "Sister, this is amazing. I just did RCP (Respiratory care), but sadly, she died. So, yes, it's so much adrenaline. You can't get that much here in Cuenca because it's much safer.

MEW: That's one way of looking at it. It's so much safer here.

LVM: I tell people to never take a taxi in Guayaquil. They're dangerous. You really have to be careful.

FLW: I did a lot of business in Mexico. I know what you're talking about. There are certain cities where you don't take taxis, certain cities where you have to bribe police, and certain cities that have underground interrogation chambers. So, yeah, I can relate. Mexico is such a beautiful country. It pays to be careful.

FLW: What do you say we begin? First, introduce yourself, and feel free to talk about anything.

LVM: I'm 32 years old. I'm a General Practitioner registered in Orthomolecular Medicine and Occupational Health. I work at the IESS (Public Hospital Jose Carrasco Arteaga) gynecology department. I love delivering babies. Coincidentally, my nephew and his wife just had baby twins yesterday. Beautiful. So, yes, I've delivered over 300 babies and plan to become a gynecologist. For every child I deliver, I place a colored ball into jars, either blue or pink, representing the child's gender.

FLW: Unusual but extraordinary.

LVM: I was in gynecology at IESS, but they reassigned me to the pandemic departments when the pandemic hit. Wow. I saw a lot of things. Stressful, having to choose who lives and who dies. Who has the best odds of living? I'm confident I made the right decisions.

FLW: So, how do you cope with that?

LVM: It was really tough. I think I got post-traumatic stress because of it.

You see patients screaming and dying; sometimes, it's out of your hands. You're not able to do anything to help them.

FLW: Did you get the support you needed?

LVM: It was challenging. So, I had to look out for myself. I had to talk to other doctors about the situation, and they could only offer advice on calming down. I got really anxious because I wanted to get everything right. *But I'm not God.* I had to deal with reality, life, and death. I had to face these decisions.

For example, there was a time when someone didn't want to go to the ICU. He didn't want to get intubated. I said, "Okay, give me five minutes." I went and changed into regular street clothes, returned to the room, and sat down next to him. I wasn't afraid of Covid. We talked about his life, wanting to see his daughter marry and enjoy grandchildren. *I listened to his story* and convinced him to go to the ICU.

FLW: Medicine is your purpose in life?

LVM: My mission is to try to save the lives I can. But sometimes, I can't because we don't have the support we need as doctors. We didn't have the oxygen, the ICU beds. So you ask yourself, what else can I do?

Sometimes, I had to go to the 8th floor, the hospital's top floor, to breathe or cry. During that time, I was apprehensive about my parents and brothers. If they got Covid, I didn't know if they could get to the hospital. So, yeah, the Covid years were hard.

FLW: I'm sorry to say that I have feelings about COVID-19's origins and geopolitics, but the horrible consequences are undeniably tragic.

MEW: I know you have a brother. How many are in your family?

LVM: Yes, I have two brothers, my Mom and Dad. A long time ago, my Dad used to work for the DEA.

FLW: I bet he has some stories. Dangerous work.

LVM: When my Mom was pregnant with me, he worked all the time. She told me there were guns and security police everywhere. Crazy.

MEW: And your Mom?

LVM: She's a professional lawyer, but she didn't practice. She stayed with us kids.

MEW: So, how did your family balance life when you were growing up?

LVM: My parents have a dairy farm about an hour outside the city with three dogs—they count as family. So, you could say we are a family of eight. They are the love of our lives.

MEW: Yes, we had three Rhodesian Ridgebacks. The love of our lives.

LVM: I love my babies.

MEW: We know Jose is a doctor. What about your other brother?

LVM: Loria, he's a lawyer here in Cuenca. He works

for the government. Jose just finished his medical internship. He's the baby. (Smiling, like older sisters are inclined to do.)

MEW: And Loria, what kind of work does he do for the government?

LVM: I don't know specifically, but it concerns property law.

MEW: So you went to school here?

LVM: I went to a private girls' school. Run by nuns.

MEW: As it happens, we're watching a Spanish show on PBS about a private girls' school in Spain. How long were you there?

LVM: Until I finished high school.

FLW: And look at you—you came out okay?!

All: [Laughter]

LVM: Thank God. You know, I have always wanted to be a doctor since I was a child. After high school, I told my parents I wanted to be a doctor. Both my Dad and Mom were shocked. They were scared for me. They were like, "Are you sure? You have to study all your life. You won't have time for boyfriends."

So I got into medical school—and they were surprised! They were astonished because they didn't think I would follow through with medicine. I had a passion for medicine. [Pausing] Funny, I would be a chef if I hadn't gotten into medicine.

FLW: Wow. A chef? Really?

LVM: Funny, huge difference, yes?

FLW: Night and day.

LVM: So, I got into a medical college and finished. It took seven years.

MEW: You went to Guayaquil for your internship?

LVM: Yes.

MEW: How long have you been practicing?

LVM: Close to eight years. It's incredible how time flies. And now my baby brother is there in the same place. My internship there was the best experience I could have had. I never went out to party. I was always at the hospital. I learned a lot. I gained a lot of experience. So that's why I told Jose to go. Now he loves it.

FLW: He's in a vibrant city.

LVM: Yeah, but I worry about him riding the motorcycle.

[Directing her to the printout]

FLW: Let's follow the printout. Tell us about your childhood.

LVM: We used to have a small farm in the jungle on the way to the Amazon. There was no town there. It was about 3 hours away. My Mom tells me we used to stay there for several weeks a year, like a vacation. It was pretty isolated. We had to leave the car 30 minutes away from the house. The house was tiny, made out of wood with a metallic roof. I remember the sound of the rain hitting the top. I used to take my books there, and the humidity would wrinkle the pages like waves. My brother and I used to catch tiny catfish in this small river. It was a beautiful experience. The sounds of the birds and the monkeys. I never got a chance to see snakes—but I love snakes!

FLW: [Cringing] Okay . . . snakes, wow.

LVM: But I'm afraid of spiders.

FLW: [Laughing] Go figure.

LVM: I loved it there. But my parents sold the farm. It was too far away.

FLW: You mentioned another farm, the dairy farm, earlier.

LVM: Yes, they bought and built a house on that farm. They did everything. The masonry. Everything. My youngest brother was only one year old when they started building the house. So, my parents became "gentlemen" farmers. It was really lovely. I used to go there a lot to visit my grandpa. [Laughing] He used to have a lot of guinea pigs.

Obviously, here in Cuenca, *we eat them*.

But my grandma has a picture of me hugging and caring for them. *She told me that because I cared for animals, I should take care of people.* I followed her advice. I was the first doctor in the family.

MEW: Your grandmother was very special to you?

LVM: Yes, very, very, special. She always encouraged me.

MEW: And other childhood memories?

LVM: Well, not so pleasant ones. I was bullied a lot by other students when I was young. I didn't have many friends because I was overweight and—*smart*. So, it was a difficult time for me. But it's over, thank God. I feel safe now. I'm doing what I love. I love being a doctor. I love delivering babies.

FLW: Are you planning on having some of your own?

LVM: Yes, I hope so! I would love to have three kids.

MEW: We only have a son. His name is Gabriel. He's about your age.

LVM: Oh, that's an adorable name.

LVM: *My family is my foundation.* I live with my parents. It's common here in Ecuador. I feel safe there.

MEW: Do you think that's changing. Generationally?

LVM: I don't think so. It's a cultural thing here. The women leave home once they get married. [In her best stern 'Mom' voice] My Mom always told me, "You will leave the house only when you get married!"

LVM: "Okay, okay . . ." I said to her. No problem. But now I'm 32.

MEW: And the clock is ticking?

LVM: Yeah, there's pressure. Many women who choose a profession are confronted with this decision. That's a critical age. You have to think about a lot of things before having a child.

FLW: I only decided to get married when I was 40. I met Mary, and I knew it was time. She was 10 years younger, so it worked out perfectly. But I understand. The timing is critical.

LVM: I know I will be the happiest woman when I have children. But it's not my time yet. It takes a lot of planning.

MEW: After Gabriel was born, I started working outside the house. Fred had a home office and took care of him. We gave Gabriel legos and a keyboard, right? He would build houses for hours at a time. He also started to play with the keyboard and computer before he was two years old. We knew what interested him. So, it was no surprise that he became a software engineer.

LVM: My Dad never imagined that I would be in medicine. My parents worried because they didn't know what I would do with my life.

FLW: Some people only know what they will do once they're 30 or 40 or older.

MEW: Did you immediately go to work at IESS?

LVM: Actually, I started working at Fundacion Hogar Del Ecuador.[1]

LVM: After that, I went to a military hospital for a year. It was the worst experience because of the culture—*a subculture.*

FLW: So it's safe to say that wasn't the best of experiences.

LVM: Terrible, here.

FLW: So you were raised on a farm? So was Mary.

MEW: We had 200 acres and fifty head of cattle. We had a forest we could walk through. We had rivers and streams, and I would return to the house when it was dark, or they would call me for dinner. I would dream under big oak trees. It was quiet. Magical.

LVM: I like what you said. Magical.

MEW: Once, my siblings and I set up a tent and camped in the woods—about a mile from the house. I woke up in the morning, and no sibling was in the tent. I was by myself, sleeping with the wild animals.

LVM: Oh, my God. They just left you there?

MEW: (Laughing) It was great. They just left me.

FLW: So, Lorena, tell us about the struggles you had to overcome.

LVM: It's difficult for a woman to become a doctor in Ecuador. It's a gender issue. You must show you're better than the men at doing certain things. Also, personally, I suffered anxiety attacks four years ago triggered by an intimate relationship. But I recovered. I'm a better person now than before.

FLW: You had to prove people wrong?

LVM: Exactly. I'm proud of myself. Empowered. I'm doing everything I want. It's great.

MEW: Good for you! You're going to attract an equally strong partner.

LVM: If you would have told me three or four years ago that I would be here at this point of my life, I wouldn't have believed it. I'm super happy.

MEW: Change happens incrementally. Step by step. Then, all of a sudden, you're there.

LVM: I agree. Sometimes, you have to struggle and learn to become successful.

FLW: So, a lot of your patients are expats?

LVM: Yes, they know me. They trust me. I began with house calls. Now everybody is doing them.

FLW: You do realize that's a foreign concept in the States? Loyal patients?

LVM: Yes, initially, when they arrive, they're vulnerable. New city, not knowing anybody or where anything is and who to contact. The learning curve is about six months.

FLW: I think even longer. We researched Cuenca for five years before moving here and were unfamiliar with many new things.

LVM: I tell my patients to just call me. I'll be there.

FLW: Even if it's in the States.

LVM: Yes, even if it's in the States. You don't leave them if they need you.

FLW: What do you consider your best accomplishments?

---

1. [*The Hogar Del Ecuador Foundation is a non-profit organization ministering to the needs of the underprivileged.*]

LVM: Believing in myself. I didn't realize the power I had. It took some time. My confidence came in stages.

FLW: Your confidence comes out in your personality. When you trust yourself, everything changes.

FLW: And how has Cuenca influenced your life?

LVM: Religion is a heavy influence in Cuenca. The people here are really religious. They go to church, to mass. They listen to the priests. My grandma just passed away. She couldn't attend church as she got older, so she used to participate in mass on TV.

Cuenca makes me appreciate architecture. Cuencanos appreciate the architecture in the city. More than other cities in Ecuador, Cuenca looks and feels like Europe—like España, doesn't it? It's gentle. You can talk to anybody if you need help; if they can help you, they do. As a matter of fact, we are going to Spain next month. At the top of the city, there's the old architecture. It's divided. Down by the river, you have modern architecture.

And the gastronomy is really changing. Improving. It's outstanding. It's becoming a "foodie" culture.

MEW: Do you have favorite restaurants?

LVM: I don't because I usually cook for myself. I shop at the Mercado. They let you taste the food before you buy it. When I get a chance, I go out. I prefer Chinese.

MEW: Really? I love Chinese. I was told that the noodle shop across the street here (San Sebastian Square) is terrific. Lamian China by the Estadio is my favorite.

FLW: You told us earlier that your Mom schedules your appointments in the States?

LVM: Yes, she's like my manager. I love to travel with her. She's experiencing more of the world. It's good for her. But I told her she needed to learn English.

[Flipping the script.]

LVM: So, what's the purpose of your book?

FLW: I hope people from different cultures can connect and learn from each other by sharing stories. Everybody's got a story, every place matters and every person matters.

LVM: So interesting. It's better when Ecuadorians tell their own stories.

FLW: Exactly. That's why we're recording.

LVM: People from the outside don't know us, right? They need to find out where Ecuador is. They think we're in Africa. They should come and visit. It's such a wonderful place with so many histories. Have you been to the cemetery under the cathedral? It's gorgeous. White marble angels.

FLW: We'll have to go. Okay, so there's a little game we like to play in these interviews and conversations. I'll give you a word. Kindly respond with the first thing that comes to mind. The first word is purpose—but I think we covered that.

FLW: How about, characters in your life?

LVM: My parents and my grandparents are real characters, definitely. My Mom is really a strong woman. Persistent. If you get knocked down, get back up. She taught that to her children. My parents have always supported me. Then there was a nun—Sister Gloria—who was really a special part of my life. Like I said earlier, I was bullied in school, and she would ask me why I was always alone at recess. She would watch me from the door. She stayed close to me to talk about my problems. I was probably eight years old. You know, I'm trying to find her to thank her. I want to give her a hug.

MEW: What order was she in?

LVM: I need to remember. I have to start doing some research. She's probably 75 or 80 years old by now. It really matters to me.

MEW: I asked about the order because as nuns get older, they move them around.

LVM: If I go to the school, they can show me pictures. She helped me a lot when I was at the school.

FLW: I had a unique, memorable character when I was young—a teacher and mentor named Jim. I had a conversation with my oldest sister, coincidentally named Gloria, and her husband Augie, and they recently had lunch with him. I was surprised he was still alive. They told me he still remembers me. I wish I could see him before he dies—to give him a hug. He meant the world to me as a child. He made a difference in my life. All it takes is one person.

LVM: Sister Gloria made me realize that only some people are right. All it takes is one person.

MEW: All it takes is one person to change a child.

LVM: So yeah, those are special characters in my life.

FLW: It's imperative if we have the chance to tell the special people in our lives how much they mean to us—before they die. My mother's brother Joe died in an auto accident when I was young.

LVM: That's so sad.

FLW: That's when I first learned to cope. I loved him. He was my friend. He would sit with me on the steps outside our front door, razz me about my piano legs, tell me jokes, and let me sip his beer. He would listen to everything I said. Sometimes, his eyes would water over when he spoke as if he knew something we didn't—

perhaps that his time was short. He would often *tell tall stories*. I remember how he'd take long, deep breaths, his barrel chest inhaling all the air in the room. I've always sensed that he knew that his life was coming to an end. He was a loveable character, authentic, down-to-earth, vulnerable and honest. Every family should have one.

LVM: Yes, sometimes all you need is someone close to you. You don't need to escape. Sometimes, you only need to know somebody is behind you. That's all the difference, right?

FLW: Absolutely. Lorena, we've touched on your goals, memorable characters, purpose, and influences. Let's go off-roading and ask you about expats. This may not be a fair question, considering your practice has much to do with expats.

LVM: You know, we're all brothers and sisters. I really love expats. When they arrive, they're vulnerable. When I meet them for the first time, I try to help them. We're all human. We have to help each other out. We're all related, right?

FLW: Right. Tell us what some of your happiest and saddest moments have been up to this point.

LVM: One of the happiest and saddest moments was when I had gastric bypass surgery. Even though I felt good about losing the weight, my struggles continued. I never felt secure, safe, or confident. I didn't love myself.

FLW: And now, how do you feel? How are you coping?

LVM: You must keep fighting with your own struggles, real or imagined. It's been 10 years since the surgery. With my family's support, I realize I have much to be grateful for. Health is the most important thing. I'm happiest when I'm working with my patients. That's the best. An unforgettable moment was when my baby brother, Jose, was born. And, of course, when Martina, my dog, had babies. She delivered 12 babies—I couldn't wait to get home from work and hold them. Unconditional love.

MEW: Our Ridgeback had babies, and we interviewed everybody who adopted them. I wish I could show you the pictures and videos. We nicknamed all of them. They all had different personalities.

FLW: Memories or regrets? What are some that stick out?

LVM: There's always some good and bad ones, right? That's part of life. I should have followed my heart more. In high school, I should have stopped the girls from bullying me. That would have made a big difference.

MEW: Don't be too hard on yourself sometimes; we're not emotionally equipped to do that at that age.

LVM: Yeah, that's a good point.

FLW: Loves?

LVM: People, animals, nature. Learning. *Learning from love.* Everyone is different from another. You always learn from what you did right and wrong.

FLW: "Learning from Love?" It could be a book title. What makes you happy and sad? Some favorite memories?

LVM: Oh, my grandma. She just passed away. It breaks my heart. At university, I used to visit with her every Friday. When I traveled, she used to call me on WhatsApp. "Are you coming?" she would ask. I was in Miami a few months ago, and she made a video and told me how much she loved me. (Laughing) She said, "I miss you so much.

Now, don't fall in love with anybody." Those memories are ones I will treasure with all my heart for a lifetime.

Not many people knew my grandma. Many people thought she was tough, but she was a sweetie. She lived a long life; she was going to be 99, but you're never prepared for the loss of somebody you loved so much. I have a video. I'm going to show you.

[Lorena pulls out her phone and plays the short video of Grandma.]

She said to me, "God helps the good people. That's why God is helping you so much."

FLW: Sharing moments makes a difference in this world, doesn't it? I mean, you have tears in your eyes.

LVM: (Sighing, her voice trailing off) "The conversations we used to have," Lorena says.

[It was the appropriate time to end the interview.]

FLW: You've overcome a lot in your life. The bullying. The gender bias. The professional hurdles. Personal losses. You should be commended for overcoming all these life-altering trials and tribulations. I know our readers will relate to your struggles and successes.

It took a lot of courage and trust to sit down and talk to us about it all. We can't thank you enough for sharing your story.

LVM: "I thought it would be a good idea because I'm an introvert.

FLW: Understood. Thanks again for trusting us.

JOSE IBANEZ'S STORY
PROMETHEUS

Rebelliously creative and innovative.

When read or heard, some individuals' life stories are etched in the sudden awareness of realization to explore the unexplored. With boundless energy and curiosity, and a fierce desire to discover the unknown such is the story of Jose Ibanez, a Spaniard from Valencia, whose restless spirit and Iberian nature propelled him across the globe only to find his heart—and future—in the warm embrace of Ecuador.

Jose is a savant, a culinary chef extraordinaire, and a marketing and food management trailblazer—all rolled into one. His story is a potent mixture of passion, determination, culture, cuisine, and an audacious sense of independence that echoes *Ralph Waldo Emerson*, the American essayist, philosopher, and champion of individualism who offered these words of wisdom:

"Do not go where the path may lead.
Go instead where there is no path and leave a trail."

Photo credit, Leonardo Duran

A nonconformist in the truest sense of the word, he embodied the demigod attributes of foresight, ingenuity, and creation. Like the Greek Titan Prometheus, who brought fire to mankind, Jose sought to infuse the culinary world with a spark of his own making.

Born in the Mediterranean hues of Valencia, Jose's journey to the Andean city of Cuenca in Ecuador was not ordinary. It was taken from an intense yearning for exploration, seasoned with an appetite for the unknown.

During this gastronomical sojourn, Jose met his future wife, attorney Magaly Rivera and the rich Ecuadorian culture and familial lifestyle that would subsequently become his own. In Cuenca, Jose found more than just a home. He found inspiration in the lush green spaces, the festive aura that constantly blew in the air, and the European architecture that carried a familiar whisper of his Valencia roots. This inspiration ultimately led him to blaze his own trail and leave his mark on the world.

Ever the independent spirit, Jose embarked on a culinary adventure that was a testament to his creativity and determination. After honing his skills in various restaurants across Ecuador, he decided to tread an uncharted path—and thus, Calvo & Co. was born. A restaurant that was an homage to his Spanish heritage stirred into the rich flavors of his adopted Ecuadorian home.

Jose's resolute spirit can be ascribed to his love for his adrenaline-fueled motorcycle riding or his youthful passion for hockey. Yes, hockey.

Yet these are but facets of his vibrant personality, the fuel that feeds his determination, the sparks that ignite his creativity. Calvo & Co. is more than just a restaurant. It is an embodiment of Jose's resilience, his cultural assimilation, and his untamed spirit. It is a shining example for those who dare to dream, a tribute to the trails blazed by a Valencian-turned-Cuencano.

Every dish served at Calvo & Co. carries a story, complex textures and nectars, and, oh, those bloody juices—a narrative of Jose's passage, testimony to his burning passion for culinary artistry, and a celebration of the cultural amalgamation that has shaped his life and work. It's a tangible memoir of a restless spirit who, against all odds, dared to embrace the unknown and create a path of his own.

Photo credit, Leonardo Duran

Photo credit, Jose Ibanez

In Jose's story, Emerson's words ring loud and clear, metaphorically guiding him through his culinary and cultural journey. Each turn in the road, every challenge faced, only solidifies Jose's belief in the significance of blazing one's own trail.

And like the Titan of lore, Jose defied the norms and brought forth blazing innovation. His is a life that celebrates individuality, embraces multicultural influences, and champions the spirit of exploration.

Such is the story of an unconventional culinary virtuoso, a tale as layered and rich as the dishes he lovingly creates, a testament to the relentless pursuit of passion and the celebration of life, culture, and cuisine.

Photo credit, Leonardo Duran

Indeed, from Valencia's vibrant streets to Cuenca's cultural melting pot, Jose has not just traveled but has created new paths. His excursion reminds us that life's richness often lies off the beaten path, where the promise of discovery fuels the restless heart, the pioneering spirit, and the Promethean fire within us all.

POSTSCRIPT

I've long harbored an emotional connection to Valencia, Spain. My conversations with Jose Ibanez reignited those feelings. The irony of meeting Jose does not escape me. Before our Ecuadorian journey, I scripted these sentiments to family and friends.

This formerly young, slender, brown-skinned boy, who grew up on a rugged, two-lane dirt road known as Valencia in the Arizona desert, has decided to spend the final chapters of his life in Valencia, Spain. This choice holds a poetic symmetry, taking him from Arizona's arid landscapes to Spain's picturesque Mediterranean coast.

Mary and I are planning our international journey, including stops in Ecuador, Chile, Argentina (specifically Patagonia), and the Iberian Peninsula (Portugal and Spain). Our preparations encompass various tasks, such as medical procedures and clearances, selling our home and cars, updating passports, obtaining extended visas, and managing residency and citizenship paperwork.

We both share a common sentiment—we've reached a point where we've had our fill. As my book series, "Escaping Culture," suggests, it's time to discover our place in the world and break free from the divisive Red/Blue political and cultural divide that characterizes so much of American society today.

We aim to reconnect with old friends and acquaintances in South America, forge new European connections, and embark on journeys wherever the winds take us. We will focus on the time we have left on this earth, savoring food and wine and experiencing the rich tapestry of different cultures.

To all our beloved family and friends, we extend a heartfelt invitation to visit us once we've settled into our new home. In fact, we insist on it. Take comfort in knowing that our chosen destinations result from hard work, a touch of serendipity, and our deep appreciation for the beauty of nature and culture.

With all due humility, I can confidently say that I was raised in Valencia, and it is here that I will ultimately rest. I wouldn't have it any other way.

JOSE IBANEZ

INTERVIEW

We conducted Jose Ibanez's interview in English and Spanish at Calvo & Co., Cuenca, Ecuador. Mary Wilson, researcher and contributor, and Leonardo Duran, translator, attended. The interview has been reconstructed from notes, audio text, translation, and recollection of conversations and edited to augment clarity.

[Abbreviations: JI: Jose Ibanez, FW: Frederico Wilson, MW: Mary Wilson, LD: Leonardo Duran.]

[Jose Ibanez approaches our table.]

FW: We sincerely thank you for graciously accepting our invitation to participate in this interview. Your willingness to engage with us is deeply appreciated, and we eagerly anticipate the opportunity to delve into meaningful dialogue with you.

JI: Before we begin. First, I would like to offer you something to drink. Something cool, a summer belt. Perhaps a glass of sangria?

FW: We're good. Thank you. Let's begin. We look forward to chronicling your journey of exploration and discovery. Share with us the story of your arrival in Ecuador.

JI: I'm 42 years old. I arrived in Quito from Valencia to visit a friend from Valencia that I had come to see. He had come to live and work with some of his friends in Ecuador.

I fell in love with this country immediately. I arrived in Quito. I got to see the city, they introduced me to some friends, and they gave me an excellent job offer as a trainer for a large catering service company.

In reality, he was offering me much more than a job. It allowed me to travel around the country because it was the largest catering company. So, it allowed me to travel around, especially the North. I had yet to learn about the South, know gastronomy, know the culture, and meet people. For me, it was an entry into a country much friendlier than any tourist or anyone who arrives and works in a closed place.

FW: As you reflect on when you arrived in Ecuador, did you realize that it was more than just a geographical location? It might have been a turning point, a leap of faith into the unknown. Did you know then that this humble beginning would shape the course of your journey in ways you never could have imagined?

JI: Yes, a few months later, I met my wife, and we began dating. We both share a passion for travel. Spending time together is something we cherish, especially considering the constraints of my job. Therefore, we decided to make the most of our free days by exploring various destinations in the North. This desire to travel together was evident from the beginning, culminating in our honeymoon trip after our marriage.

Instead of heading to Cancun, we rendezvoused in the southern region of Ecuador, an unfamiliar destination. My wife hails from Santa Cruz de Galapagos; she departed the Galapagos to pursue her studies at university and settle in Quito. Upon her arrival in the capital, we decided to make it our home.

Exploring the customs and traditions of the places you visit becomes much easier through catering, as it entails more than just showing up and serving individuals. It requires a deeper understanding of the client's needs. Take some time to explore your options to meet those needs better.

When we got married, we decided to explore the South of Ecuador since we had yet to go. Our journey led us to Machala, Loja, and Arenillas (Ecuador), where we embarked on a honeymoon tour. Upon reaching Cuenca,

we were captivated by its charm at first sight.

Cuenca retains the ambiance of a close-knit community where everyone knows each other, reminiscent of bygone eras. This quaint aspect and architecture are reminiscent of my homeland and to its allure. The resemblance to Valencia is striking.

We left our jobs, secured an apartment, and purchased a house in Cuenca without any prior acquaintances in the area. Through the kindness of a friend in Quito, we were introduced to someone who facilitated our initial days here. Thus, we began to acquaint ourselves with our new surroundings.

He helped us get to know the city a little. He helped us find the house because we needed help finding a suitable home. Luckily, a friend of this man was an acquaintance of the architect who was building our house for me, so we bought our house without having finished it.

Thanks to this individual, we were introduced to the proprietors of Dos Chorreras Inn in Alcázar. They extended a job offer to me, prompting my appointment as the establishment's manager. I dedicated two years to this role until I was unfortunately afflicted with a lung disease.

I resigned from my previous position, and shortly thereafter, I was offered the manager position at the Santa Barbara Hotel in Guarapeo. After a year in that role, I was allowed to become the manager of the Golden Prague.

MW: The Golden Prague in El Vergel, Cuenca?

JI: Yes, there was a bridge between the Inn, The Golden Prague, and establishing my own business. Here, the notion of working for myself rather than continually enriching others took root. Ultimately, investing in work that falls on deaf ears yields little return compared to working for oneself.

I noticed a significant gap in the market—a lack of gourmet sandwiches. No one in this country seemed to be making gourmet sandwiches. I searched for diverse dining options but couldn't find what I wanted, hence, when I contemplated starting my own business.

I decided to fill the gap by introducing a gourmet sandwich concept absent from the market. My initial menu comprised five sandwiches and two burgers—our entire offering. As people began sampling our creations, they preferred our burgers over sandwiches. Responding to this demand, we expanded our burger line. Within a year, our dedication paid off, and we were honored with the Best Gringo Post Hamburger Award.

The recognition came from the frequent visits of our clientele, some returning up to three times a week. This consistent patronage underscored our success, prompting us to delve into customer preferences and needs. We initiated a process of evaluation, actively soliciting feedback to discern what our patrons desired. This led us to innovate, introducing new options and instituting a crucial feature: the "Special of the Month."

Our establishment now proudly cultivates a tradition centered on the monthly special dish. Each month brings a unique culinary creation distinct from our regular menu offerings. Customers have come to anticipate this novelty, knowing that with the turn of each calendar page, they can expect a fresh culinary experience. Whether they visit frequently or infrequently, they can rely on the assurance that our offerings will consistently evolve.

FW: Over time, you methodically broadened your range of menu offerings to meet the demands of your clientele. You transformed your menu into a dynamic reflection of your commitment to culinary excellence and customer satisfaction.

JI: Exactly. We've recently expanded our menu offerings to cater to our customers' requests better. One notable addition is our authentic *paella*, a dish native to my hometown of Valencia, Spain.

One day, I decided to bring along a friend—a highly skilled chef residing in Tumbes, although he hails from Spain. This friend of mine has been my colleague for years, both in Valencia and Peru. Having settled in Tumbes after marrying a local, he decided to open a restaurant here.

As the 2019 Cuenca festivities approached, I invited my friend to join me for a paella festival. This event, spanning three days, was our most significant endeavor yet. During this time, we successfully sold over 500 paella servings, catering to restaurant patrons and take-out customers.

Reflecting on the event, we marveled at the contrast with our previous venue, which could only accommodate 30 guests. The demand for paella was so overwhelming that we prepared it continuously for practically 20 consecutive days, with only brief breaks. Each day felt like a blur of non-stop paella preparation, with the clang of our two enormous paella pans.

MW: And now, with the addition of Flamenco dancing to your paella events, you've added to the cultural tapestry of Cuenca. The paella gatherings are very popular.

FW: Transitioning to family-related matters, tell us a little about your family, faith, and childhood.

JI: I was born into a working-class family where my parents held jobs. During my early years, my father served as a salesman for a furniture brand, a role he played with significance on a national scale in Spain. He was a merchant. Meanwhile, my mother worked as a nurse at a hospital. I've seen the passing of both my parents.

My father departed this world 11 years ago, and my mother just a year ago. It's been a time of reflection, and I've placed my faith in it. Although raised in the Catholic tradition, I've not actively practiced it for years. After my first communion, I gradually ceased attending Church. There was no pressure from my parents, just as I haven't compelled my children to attend Church.

While I've been baptized and received communion, my connection to organized religion waned over time. I still believe in a higher power, but I've grown skeptical of those who claim authority over interpreting and conveying the divine message.

MW: How did your initial curiosity about other countries evolve, eventually leading you to embark on journeys of exploration and travel?

JI: I've traveled extensively within my country with friends, girlfriends, brothers, and family. However, the most unforgettable journey was when I ventured beyond my country's borders to another continent. It was my first trip outside of the continent. I had only traveled to France and only ventured within the continent's borders. My first flight on a plane took me directly to South America. It proved to be a memorable journey.

FW: Relocating to another country involves immersion into a new culture, which invariably fosters growth, understanding, and introspection. Did you find yourself reevaluating your perspectives and gaining a deeper appreciation for cultural diversity?

JI: Somewhat. Let me explain. A few months ago, I experienced a severe motorcycle accident. Despite being an enthusiast of motorcycle riding and owning a Harley, my perspective shifted when I was introduced to the mountain trails of dual-purpose biking. Captivated by the annual Andes Motorcycle Challenge rally, I eagerly participated in March or April—I can't recall precisely. The rally led me through an indigenous community in Tena, Ecuador, where I crossed the Amazon rainforest. My adventure took a dangerous turn as I lost control, and my motorcycle flipped twice, throwing me into a ditch.

Somehow, I escaped severe injury, except for a lingering ringing in my ears, a common aftermath of head trauma. I managed to evade major harm thanks to the rupture of my hydration backpack upon impact, which cushioned my fall.

Luckily, a friend who happened to be a race volunteer aided me, leading to an unexpected spiritual encounter. I was shocked when asked to attend a closing ceremony because I was skeptical of spiritual retreats and religion. Witnessing fanatical testimonies, I initially dismissed the experience as individuals surrendering critical thinking for blind faith.

Despite my disinterest in organized religion, I was strangely drawn to the Bible. Gradually, I've come to acknowledge a divine presence in my life, although I don't preach or proselytize.

Since then, conversations with friends have revealed

hidden facets of their lives, surprising me with revelations of their spiritual journeys. In retrospect, my accident stripped away my skepticism, revealing new perspectives.

FW: So, in essence, you experienced an epiphany—an awakening, some might say, a "come-to-Jesus moment." These instances frequently prompt further realizations, such as accepting the weight of our struggles, failures, and successes.

JI: My struggles and my successes have been intertwined throughout my life. At 18, I became a father, and now, at 24, my oldest son and I have not lived together since his early years. The challenges were evident from the start—being a young, inexperienced father without fully understanding my responsibilities.

The separation from my son's mother when he was just a year and a half old compounded these struggles. Later, I remarried and had another son, only to face a similar situation of separation when he was also a toddler. It seems fate has challenged my role as a father repeatedly, leaving me hesitant to pursue it further. Marriage, particularly in the Church, wasn't something I had considered until recently, despite being married for seven years. It wasn't part of the plan, but now I contemplate it.

As for my successes, they've been more about achieving personal goals than material accomplishments. Joining the military was a childhood dream that I fulfilled, yet it didn't bring the satisfaction I expected. Similarly, becoming a restaurant manager was a goal I achieved but didn't consider a true success.

True success came when I met my wife. With her, I found happiness and completeness I hadn't experienced before. Our relationship brought harmony and fulfillment that had been missing in my previous undertakings.

Beyond these milestones, every day presents vital experiences. From overcoming the loss of loved ones to exploring new places and cultures, each moment shapes who I am and offers growth opportunities. Ultimately, success is not measured solely by material gains but by the richness of life experiences and the ability to positively impact others.

Rising each morning to embrace a new opportunity is a transformative experience. I've encountered many diverse moments, each influencing and guiding me. Each experience has enriched my journey, from immersing myself in the culture of communities guided by a shaman to witnessing the awe-inspiring majesty of The Pailón Del Diablo waterfall in Banos, Ecuador.[1]

FW: I understand. Like the sightseeing mentioned, such moments transcend simplicity to touchstones in life. The essence lies in the renewal of purpose and the desire to extend a helping hand to others.

JI: But achieving your goals is mainly within your control. Upon arriving in Ecuador, I recognized the fortunate circumstances in which I found myself. Being Spanish, I possess fluency in the language, hold a Spanish passport, and thus have the privilege of accessing nearly any destination worldwide.

MW: Could you elaborate on how your goals may have evolved or shifted since your arrival in Ecuador? What factors or experiences have influenced any changes

---

1. *Awe-inspiring and breathless, the Devil's Cauldron waterfall is located in Banos, Ecuador.*

in your aspirations or objectives during your time in the country?

JI: I am a basic person. I find contentment in simple things. My primary aspiration? Happiness. It's the light that guides my life journey. I love to travel and explore new lands and cultures. It's part of my identity.

FW: Throughout your journey, you must have encountered some memorable characters. Is there anyone in particular you'd like to discuss?

JI: My dad is the most memorable person; he taught me everything. However, I don't have anyone in particular. You must understand I don't have a favorite rock band, artist, or best friend; I have many best friends. I strive not to harbor enemies; it's better to trust and believe in the goodness of people. Every person who has crossed paths with me has contributed something valuable and taught me lessons. Through experience, one learns the importance of listening and understanding.

FW: Looking ahead, what do you envision for your future? What aspirations are guiding your plans and goals?

JI: When I turn fifty, I have a plan. I want to open smaller restaurants outside of Cuenca. As you know, Cuenca is complex and highly competitive. To thrive here, one must establish a reputation. It's more like a large town than a big city.

FW: In other words, it's a tough nut to crack.

JI: Please understand me: Cuenca has afforded me many opportunities. However, we're also exploring investments in other smaller cities, and, of course, we want to travel more. *I want to know more about the world.*

For example, you know, when you leave the city, you meet people in extreme poverty. Initially, you may fear they'll harm you. But in reality, they're often more afraid of you than you are of them. They want to help you. It's often *the person with the least who gives the most*—to those who need it most.

FW: It all has a philosophical bent to it.

JI: As someone who didn't study the subject, I perceive philosophy as something embraced by individuals whose perspectives evolved. In my youth, I saw no purpose in studying philosophy. However, with age, I've come to appreciate its role in preserving past wisdom.

FW: Philosophy prompts us to reflect on historical events, preventing their loss. This is how I understand its contribution to the world.

JI: Yes, but it's a quest that doesn't sustain us. Who would engage in something that doesn't nourish them? This dilemma is personal to me. I lack a direct connection with a mentor; my grandparents and mother passed away when I was young. This realization struck me when my mother died, leaving behind unresolved questions about her life. My brother, acting as her caretaker during her illness, gave her a book filled with questions, essentially a template for her memoirs. Reflecting on this, I acknowledge the difficulty in confronting these memories. The book represents my mother's untold story, a narrative I struggle to complete due to overwhelming emotions. It's a poignant reminder of cherishing and understanding our parents.

FW: You've just created a compelling case for why everyone should write a memoir. There's value in self-reflection and preserving history. Sharing a message—a story—contributes to the collective narrative of humanity, of us all.[2]

MW: In exploring your motivations and daily routines, I'm interested in understanding what drives you forward and how you structure your time to achieve your goals. Could you provide insights into the factors that inspire and energize you and paint a picture of the typical activities, tasks, and rituals that shape your day-to-day life?

JI: I start my day by waking up at 6:45 every morning. Since I begin work early, I must attend to my two dogs and two cats as my wife leaves for work before dawn. By 8 o'clock, I'm heading to the bank. My day is consumed by work and errands, leaving little time for leisure. Nonetheless, I prioritize spending time with my wife, my daily inspiration for self-improvement. My children also motivate me to strive for excellence, daily pushing me to become a better father. Above all, my ultimate motivation is to achieve my goals, no matter how challenging they may seem. I refuse to accept defeat easily. Once I set my mind on something, I achieve it. This commitment is my primary motivation, pushing me forward even in the face of adversity.

FW: As you reflect on this current stage of your life, do you have any regrets or moments of contemplation about choices made or paths not taken? Considering the experiences and lessons learned thus far, are there aspects of your journey that you wish you had approached differently, and if so, what insights have you gained from these reflections?

JI: I regret not pursuing specific opportunities but don't regret my choices. There are limitations to what we can achieve as time passes. For instance, I might have considered a different career path, but starting early when I was young was essential. Despite my desire to explore various paths, one ambition lingered: to serve in the military.

Later, I opted to join the rescue team. The thought of aiding others and making a positive difference has always appealed to me. It's a sentiment I hold dear. I wish I had pursued it sooner instead of veering off in other directions. Nevertheless, I have no regrets for my decisions, flawed though they may have been.

FW: How about when you were younger?

JI: In my youth, I was sometimes reckless, and I find moments embarrassing when looking back. However, those experiences shaped who I am today. What truly weighs on me are the missed opportunities for more meaningful activities. Regrettably, I didn't prioritize spending time with my son during his formative years. In my later years, I lament the moments I didn't share with

---

2. I've said this before in earlier writings, but it's worth mentioning about losing loved ones and the impact it has on us. "Neither science nor philosophy nor religion answers the mystery of why we're here, why and when we die, and where we go after our demise. The more we think we know, the more questions there are than answers. Ambiguity insulates us from ourselves, from our inability to cope with revelations we're ill-prepared to handle. Perhaps we learn to live life in the face of loss. Perhaps our life isn't about us at all but more about what we leave behind. In the interim, we muddle through, hoping that revelations from whatever source provides us clues in our pursuit of reason."

my parents. The absence of these experiences haunts me most. In this regard, *I regret the paths I didn't take.*[3]

MW: I get the impression that you're not prone to panic, but clearly, you're a sensitive man. Is there anything that makes you anxious, something you fear the most?

JI: I'm not afraid of many things. I recommend being alone and embracing the unknown. I enjoy solitude and time, but I fear the uncertainty of being alone and not knowing how to enjoy it. Everything happens for a reason, and I'm not afraid of what that reason may be.

FW: Uncertainty is a common experience many individuals share, although only some readily accept it. Grappling with uncertainty is part of life's journey. Let's imagine someone is seeking insight into who you are as an individual and a business person. What would you say to that person?

JI: I will share a brief story reflecting who I am as a person. When I started my business, I had limited resources, just my savings. This gives you an idea of how modest our cash reserves were, including what was in the cash register for making change. I launched the business without partners and only a small loan. I recall the moment when the loan was approved. It was essential, coinciding with the arrival of our largest group of customers yet. Initially, we rented a space next to an empty lot to expand. One day, as I was working, cotton-like pollen from nearby trees began to fall, covering the ground. I swept the mess, needing a vacuum or blower. I served

as my waiter, managing all tasks single-handedly. When a friend suggested I invest in cleaning equipment, I explained I needed to prioritize expenses, like installing a door in our new rental space.

So anyway, upon finishing their meal, a customer approached me to settle the bill, offering $300 in support. I declined, explaining that their patronage and referrals were the most valuable support I could ask for.

My refusal moved him, and tears came to his eyes. He said he admired my integrity. That moment remains one of the most cherished memories of my life.

FW: That speaks volumes. Upon your arrival from Spain, what were your initial impressions of Ecuadorians? Could you elaborate on the cultural nuances and differences you noticed?

JI: Let me put this into context. Many foreigners have preconceived notions of what Ecuador and its people are like. For instance, those from the United States often carry with them the stereotype of Ecuadorians as poor and less educated, based on the early Ecuadorian migrants.

However, when they arrive in Cuenca, they are surprised to find a diverse population of people of various appearances, education, and backgrounds. It becomes clear that most migrants do not fit the unfavorable impression made by the first wave of emigrants.

The initial Ecuadorian migrants to Spain were predominantly perceived as of low socio-economic sta-

---

3. *During this part of the interview, I drew parallels between 'The Paths Jose Didn't Take' and 'The Road Not Taken' by American poet Robert Frost. In Frost's poem, he illustrates a person standing at a crossroads in the woods, uncertain about which path to choose. This metaphor symbolizes life's journey and the significance of our decisions, akin to a fork in the road.*

tus, spreading the stereotype of Ecuador as a disorderly country. However, this perception needs to reflect the reality of Ecuador as a nation rich in culture, education, and beauty. Cuenca, in particular, stands out as a clean, orderly, and architecturally stunning city, boasting a vibrant cultural scene and a strong sense of community. This positive image of Ecuador is often overshadowed by the negative stereotypes perpetuated by the first migrants, but it is essential to recognize and celebrate the true essence of the country.

Another thing is that the generational gap between older and younger Ecuadorians also plays a role in perpetuating stereotypes. Older adults tend to hold onto preconceived notions about other cultures, making it difficult to change their opinions. On the other hand, younger generations are more susceptible to influence, mainly through online media. It can be both a blessing and a curse, allowing for easy manipulation of beliefs. Raising understanding and respect between different generations and cultures is critical to breaking down stereotypes and building meaningful connections.

FW: I believe that's called raising consciousness.

JI: In Spain, respect is culturally important, particularly towards elders and those in positions of authority. However, this respect should not be misinterpreted as distance or formality. For example, addressing someone as "tu" (you) rather than "usted" is not a sign of disrespect but rather a sign of familiarity and a desire to form a closer connection. It's important to understand because it shows warmth in relationships. So, regardless of age or status, the ultimate goal is to build honest friendships and nurture mutual trust and understanding.

FW: I agree wholeheartedly. I still get the impression you miss your homeland and culture.

JI: Cuenca is home. But yes, I will always miss my culture, my land. I will probably retire there. You see, here, it's tough for the elderly to live well. An older adult cannot cross the street because cars will not stop. They'll run you over, right?

MW: (Laughing) Yes, it's definitely a different driving culture.

JI: Wherever I retire, I will live in the countryside.

FW: We have that in common. And on that note, we can retire, pardon the pun, this very enlightening conversation. Your experiences in this city have undoubtedly shaped your worldview, personal beliefs, empathy, and appreciation for cultures. I truly appreciate your sincerity and honesty. People are only sometimes willing to open up about their journeys.

JI: So when the book is finished, I want to put it on display here at the restaurant. I'm looking forward to reading the other people's stories you interviewed. Congratulations on an excellent idea for the book. Enjoy your meal. It was very nice to meet you.

FW: My pleasure, Jose. Thank you once again.

PHOTOGRAPHS

THE JEFF SCHINSKY COLLECTION

Photo credit, Jeff Schinsky

Photograph credit, Jeff Schinksy

Alpacas
A farm outside of Nabon, one hour south of Cuenca

Photo credit, Jeff Schinsky

Rio Tomebamba, taken at Parque Lineal alongside Avendida Roma.

Photo credit, Jeff Schinsky

Stream at covered bridge on the road between the Cajas highway
and Laguna Llaviucu, El Cajas National Park.

Photo credit, Jeff Schinsky

Rio Tomebamba with view of Iglesia Todos Santos,
taken from Puente de Todos Santos.

Photo credit, Jeff Schinsky

Rio Yanuncay, alongside Avenida 27 de Febrero
and Station House #3 of Los Bomberos.

Photo credit, Jeff Schinsky

Plaza Civica, behind Mercado 9 de Octubre, Cuenca.

Photo credit, Jeff Schinsky

Illuminated "Navidad" sign in Parque Calderon, Cuenca.

Photo credit, Jeff Schinsky

Rio Tomebamba, taken from Puente de Todos Santos.

Photo credit, Jeff Schinsky

Church steps in Zaruma, Ecuador, leading down to Calle Bolivar.
Church name: Santuario Catolico Nuestra Senora del Carmen.

Photo credit, Jeff Schinsky

Early evening view of Zaruma, Ecuador.

Photo credit, Jeff Schinsky

Alcaldia de Cuenca (with the flags),
Presidente Borrero y Simon Bolivar.

Photo credit, Jeff Schinsky

La Escalinata taken from near Calle Larga and Hermano Miguel, Cuenca.

Photo credit, Jeff Schinsky

Puente Roto, between Calle Larga and the Tomebamba River.

Photo credit, Jeff Schinsky

Puente Roto, Calle Larga and the Tomebamba River.

Photo credit, Jeff Schinsky

Parque Calderon, Cuenca, Ecuador.

Photo credit, Jeff Schinsky

Garden behind the restaurant plaza that runs alongside
Catedral de la Inmaculada Concepcion,
Padre Aguirre y Simon Bolivar.

Llamas and Alpacas at Laguna Llaviucu, El Cajas National Park.

Photo credit, Jeff Schinsky

Laguna Toreadora, El Cajas National Park.

Photo credit, Jeff Schinsky

View from Laguna Llaviucu,
El Cajas National Park.

Catedral de la Inmaculada Concepcion and Cuenca's Centro Historico,
taken from Turi.

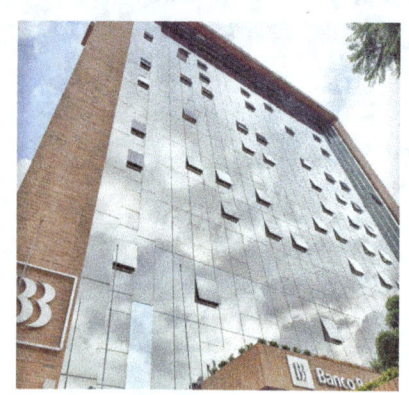

(clockwise from top left)

Edificio Montano—Offices, Condos
Edificio Montano—Offices, Condos
Sheraton Four Points Hotel—Next to Mall del Rio
Conjunto Residencial Vistalinda Condos
Camara de Industrias—Office Building
Edificio Acropolis—Medical, Office Building
Camara de Comercio de Cuenca—Office Building
Edificio Atlantida Condos
Edificio Onix—Office Building

YOUTH

I'm older than dirt. So I've had the opportunity in my lifetime to travel extensively to gain some insights. One of the things I've enjoyed most is observing the characteristics shared in different generations of young people from different cultures. Here are a few of my thoughts.

Youth is a period of exploration and discovery. Young people constantly seek new experiences, push boundaries, and expand their horizons. This spirit of adventure leads to personal growth, diverse skills, and knowledge acquisition. The willingness to explore the unknown is a virtue that ultimately drives innovation and progress.

Youth think outside the box. It's a time of creativity and resourcefulness. The young are not constrained by convention, making them adept at finding innovative solutions to problems. Whether it's a digital hackathon or leveraging technology for everyday challenges, the resourcefulness and energy of youth know no bounds.

It's easy to stereotype youth as easily distracted in today's digital age. However, many possess an impressive level of focus. When young people are passionate about something, they concentrate their energy and efforts on that goal. This razor focus often leads to achievements in various fields, from academics and business to sports and entrepreneurship.

The impatience of youth is often viewed negatively but can also prove to be a virtue. Young people's impatience stems from their desire for change and progress. More often than not, they refuse to accept the status quo and are eager to challenge the norms. This impatience with how things are often leads to activism, the pursuit of justice, and social change, making it a powerful force for positive transformation.

One of youth's most endearing virtues is their earnestness. Young people approach life with wide-open eyes, enthusiasm, sincerity, and a genuine belief that they can make a difference. This unwavering conviction in their abilities and the potential for positive change is a driving force that can inspire and lead to remarkable endeavors.

Youth is an age of an individual's lifespan characterized by limitless energy, curiosity, and a voracious appetite for knowledge and social and work experiences. It's a period marked by discovery, resourcefulness, focus, earnestness, and impatience. They're unique to this age group. The qualities or the virtues of youth contribute to the progress and betterment of society. As a society, we should support and mentor their development. After all, they will shape the future for us all.

I've been fortunate to connect with numerous young individuals in Cuenca. I want to thank Isabel, Jonnathan, Antonella, and Mateo for their candidness, trust, and bravery in sharing their stories. They intended to demonstrate to our readers that, in essence, we're all quite similar. As young people worldwide, we all have similar characteristics, obstacles, and aspirations.

ISABEL CASAJOANA'S STORY
THE ARCHER

Sometimes, whether by force or chance—fate seeks you out. Sometimes, it comes calling in the middle of the night. Sometimes, through no fault of your own, your fate is a consequence of culture, heritage, and chance.

As I sat across from Isabel, her story unfolded before me, revealing a remarkable journey intertwined with the art of archery. In my mind's eye, I pictured Isabel as a resolute figure, firmly grounded with an unwavering posture. Her eyes bore the unmistakable combination of determination and tranquility. Cradled in her hands was a longbow, an embodiment of grace and strength. One hand pulled back the string poised to release an arrow into the unknown. Her stance, flawless and precise, illustrated her prowess and extensive training.

The skills associated with the bow and arrow served as a metaphor for her pursuit of purpose and achievement in life. Drawing a bow, releasing an arrow, and hitting one's targets (goals) requires concentration, precision, and control. And if there's one attribute you glean from spending time with Isabel, *its focus.* Archery taught her to live in the present and trust her instincts to pursue life goals.

Illustration credit, Catalina Carrasco

Photo credit, Isabel Casajoana

My wife, Mary, and I had the pleasure of meeting Isabel at a hotel in Cuenca, where she was the manager. Our interview with her occurred many months later in a downtown eatery, coinciding with a local indigenous peoples' strike, a "Paro," protesting various social and economic injustices. During this encounter, we began to glimpse the depths of Isabel's character.

There's much more to be said of this young lady. A proud descendant of one of Cuenca's founding families (Ordonez), she exudes the confidence one would expect from generational guidance and legacy without the hauteur typically associated with social standing.

Her great-great-grandmother, Hortensia Mata de Ordonez, was an extraordinary figure in Ecuador's history. A philanthropist and businesswoman, she earned the title of "First Lady of Cuenca" due to her profound influence on the political, economic, and cultural landscape of the late 19th and early 20th centuries. Hortensia was wed to Jose Miguel Ordonez Lazo, a wealthy businessman, and together, they amassed a substantial fortune by exporting quinine, cocoa husks, and Panama hats. Their real estate holdings, strategically situated in and around Parque Calderon, the heart of Cuenca, further solidified their economic prowess.

Their union was blessed with an astonishing 16 children, a testament to their prosperity and influence. The Ordonez Mata family tree extended its branches throughout Ecuador, yielding influential local, regional, and national political and economic figures. It included past governors of the Canton/Provincia Del Azuay and influential members of the Catholic Church.

The conversations with Isabel unfolded in the historic Casa Del Parque, also known as the Mansion Matilde. This remarkable building, at the intersection of Luis Cordero and Simon Bolivar Ave., was initially constructed around 1880 and belonged to the Ordonez Mata family. Over the years, it witnessed the city's major political and social events, making it the epicenter of Cuenca's illustrious history. At the time, it was the only establish-

Photo credit, Frederico Wilson

Hortensia Mata de Ordonez

Hortensia Mata Lamota was born in Guayaquil in 1849. She was an Ecuadorian businesswoman and philanthropist. She was considered the FIRST LADY OF CUENCA due to her political, economic, and cultural influence. —Wikipedia https://en.wikipedia.org/wiki/Hortensia_Mata

Her daughter, Rosa, was Isabel's great-grandmother's mother (Lucrecia Moscoso Ordonez)

ment suitable for accommodating esteemed guests, symbolizing the Ordonez family's enduring legacy.

Ultimately, Isabel's story is a testament to the power of destiny, culture, heritage, and chance. Through her archery, she embodies the essence of focus, determination, and precision, reflecting the journey of an individual whose fate is intricately woven into the tapestry of her family's rich history and the city of Cuenca itself.

As we parted ways, I couldn't help but marvel at how her family's legacy, much like the arrow she so skillfully wields, continues to pierce through the fabric of time, leaving an indomitable mark on the pages of history.

With that introduction as a prologue, the interview follows.

ISABEL CASAJOANA

INTERVIEW

The interview with Isabel Casajoana occurred at "Sofy Glocal Cuisine" in Parque Calderon, Cuenca, Ecuador. Mary Wilson, a researcher and contributor, participated in the interview. The text has been reconstructed from interview notes, audio, and recollection of conversations and edited to augment clarity.

[Abbreviations: IC: Isabel Casajoana, FW: Frederico Wilson, MW: Mary Wilson]

[Having already reintroduced ourselves Mary and Isabel discuss the "Paro" (Strike/Stoppage) in previous years.]

IC: We had similar strikes (Paros) in 2019. There was a lot more distraction in the city center. This time, the President didn't want to give in. In 2019, it lasted about a week. We witnessed strikes, people throwing rocks, destroying buildings, and hurling tear gas. The streets were filled with police. This time around, the situation was less destructive.

MW: People are saying we will have another protest on the 21st.

IC: I'm sure they will try to find solutions before it happens. The government wants to make everybody happy. There's a big issue about how gas subsidies are collected and distributed. The subsidies needed to be fairly distributed to the middle class. It was a tiered system, and the middle class paid a progressive tax based on their annual salary. Everybody has to pay currently, but the people making minimum wage don't have to.

MW: What's the minimum wage in Cuenca?

IC: Currently? $425 per month.

MW: The visa requirement is tied to the monthly wage. It was $400 per month; now, it's $425. The requirements keep changing, which needs to be clarified. And before, if you had a visa, you could leave for 22 months, but now it's been reduced to 90 days.

IC: Well, what was happening? People were coming

here, getting their visas, banking CDs with high interest rates, and then leaving. *They weren't spending any money.*

FW: Without feeling pressured or uncomfortable, given the importance of diversity in Cuenca, it's essential to understand diverse perspectives and experiences. With that in mind, we'd like to ask about your racial or ethnic background. Please feel free to share whatever you're comfortable with, as we're interested in learning more about the unique perspectives and insights you can offer. Your response will help us foster an understanding of Cuencanos. Let's begin with your family.

IC: My great-grandfather, who is on my father's side, is from Barcelona, Spain. My grandfather, who was on my mother's side, was born in Quito. My mother is related to Hortensia Mata Lamota.

MW: We've seen her portraits in different businesses throughout Parque Calderon.

IC: She is known as the "First Lady of Cuenca." She married Jose Miguel Ordonez Lazo, and they became wealthy by exporting quinine and Panama hats. They built most of the French buildings in El Centro and throughout Cuenca.

MW: So help me out here. How many generations are you removed from Hortensia?

IC: Hortensia's daughter Rosa, I believe, is my great-grandmother's mother, Lucrecia Moscoso Ordonez.

FW: You lost me, but I get the meaning. There's a direct ancestral line to the primary founder of Cuenca.

IC: She had a ton of kids. I believe 16 or 17. It's funny because they're probably related if you ask anybody in the middle class here.

MW: You better be careful who you date and marry in Cuenca.

IC: Yes, my twin brothers followed their Spanish bloodlines and moved to Europe. They lived in Germany for the past 12 years. Although one of them moved to Utah, but has decided to move to Spain to be closer to my other brother.

MW: So, do you go visit your brothers?

IC: Yes, I love to travel, especially to Europe. I love it.

MW: How old are your brothers?

IC: Thirty-one. I'm 34, *much older.*

ALL: Laughter.

MW: Same as our son, Gabriel. He just got married two weeks ago.

IC: Guests keep trying to introduce me to their kids. Finally, one worked out. I'm dating him, but he lives in California.

FW: Long distance relationship. That takes work.

IC: I'm going to see him in a couple of weeks. He works at a University in central California.

MW: Earlier, you mentioned Switzerland.

IC: Yes, I studied gastronomy there. I went to culinary school, worked in kitchens, and owned a catering business for a while. But then I decided I didn't want to work in the kitchen anymore. It was terrible. Gastronomy is gender-based. A lot of issues. When I returned from Switzerland, a friend asked me to help him restructure kitchens. It was challenging. It was tough to get males and coworkers to respect me. And, of course, when something went wrong, it was always my fault.

FW: Did you find the same gender issues in Europe as in Ecuador?

IC: There's a little more respect for women in Europe and the United States—but not much. So, I decided to make a career change and moved into the hospitality industry.

MW: Where, when and how did you learn English?

IC: English is mandatory in Cuenca schools. Private schools are better than public. There's even a German school here.

FW: You traveled to Germany, it must have helped you. Your brothers must be fluent by now.

IC: I'm trying to pick it up again. One of my brothers has forgotten most of it because he doesn't have anyone to practice with but my dad has been in Germany for 15 years and speaks fluently.

MW: So you attended the local German high school?

IC: I graduated from there. Then I went to culinary school. I graduated from there. Started working, and then went to Switzerland to study hospitality.

FW: You're driven. Did you inherit that from your parents?

IC: My dad's a mechanical engineer, a machine designer. He associates little with people. Everything is physics and math. And my mother worked in finance at the university until she married and had children. I think my drive comes from my studying psychology. I find it tough to see people suffer from mental illnesses and I felt that I would like to help people. I like to make people happy and that's probably why I transitioned into customer service and the hospitality industry.

FW: Isabel, let me clarify the purpose of the interviews we're conducting. By compiling this project into a book, we aim to highlight cultural variances. Our goal is to unite people through understanding, right? Individual stories provide a sense of unity as they showcase commonalities, regardless of origin. That's our intention with this specific book. That's where we're coming from. Now, you briefly mentioned your family and parents.

IC: Oh, my parents are great! They've instructed us to become good individuals without imposing the requirement to be good. This is essential. When my dad was a child, he tragically lost his mother, which stressed the importance of family to him. Consequently, he made efforts to nurture family closeness. We keep regular communication with my brothers despite our geographical separation. Also, my mother tries to stay connected with her siblings, making sure that family bonds remain strong.

MW: We've discovered that the importance of family is a common theme in Cuenca.

IC: Yes, our family's gatherings for meals and various activities were commonplace, a tradition since childhood. Weekends were meant for family reunions, where we would meet our cousins, either cooking together or ordering takeout if the occasion called for it.

Even though most of my cousins are older than me, we share connections and relationships and appreciate the memories we've shared despite the age gap. Our obligation to family unity goes beyond generational differences and is important to each of us. So my family is together all of the time.

When I first visited Barcelona, I knew a part of my family was from there, but I never expected the deepness of the connection. I truly felt at home. I understood what my brother experienced when he arrived in Europe. He was comfortable and blossomed. There's an intense connection, something I want to explore further.

While in Switzerland, I had the opportunity to live with people from many different cultures because the community was diverse. Discovering our similarities while appreciating our differences was terrific, enriching our experiences to learn and share.

FW: In my writings, I've frequently emphasized breaking free from cultural confines to truly embrace and appreciate other cultures.

IC: That's what happened in my situation. My father has always been open to embracing other cultures. Despite leaving Ecuador during his teenage years, he retains a deep-rooted connection to Ecuador. This influence inspires us to remain open-minded and connected to our roots. I am committed to appreciating people from various cultural backgrounds. I actively seek opportunities to learn from them, share their traditions, and compare them with mine. I had a Salvadoran friend in Switzerland. We shared stories, traditions, and secrets, and whenever necessary, we took the time to explain and clarify any misunderstandings.

MW: I've noticed that people in Ecuador have started to lose their traditions.

IC: Do you know why? Our society is evolving and increasingly influenced by Western and Northern cultures.

FW: I suspect it also involves the impact of global trends and technologies, leading to a shift in lifestyles and values.

IC: And generational changes.

MW: Young and old. As older people pass away, they take with them traditions and customs.

FW: And, of course, the ever-changing economics, educational opportunities, and commercial media influences. Here in Ecuador, you're confronted with environmental and social changes that force communities to change cultural practices.

Switching subjects, let's talk about challenges, difficulties, and obstacles in your life.

IC: Believe it or not, my choice of the hospitality industry has made it difficult for me to socialize with people. I value solitude, moments of patience, and self-reflection.

MW: I never would have guessed. You took such good care of us. As foreigners entering another country, we were like lost babes in the wilderness. So, you were highly available in the first month and met every need. You would point us in the right direction. You were very, very good. I never would have guessed that you were an introvert.

IC: As a manager of Grand Colombia Suites, I find great satisfaction in my role. Despite its challenges, building relationships with our guests is something I genuinely treasure. Our guests aren't just passing through for a night or two; many stay for months or years, becoming members of our extended family. It would feel odd for me to retreat to my office and refrain from engaging with them. They are an essential part of our home and community.

I think I got this from my dad. He wanted us to be open to everything. We grew up with diverse tastes: music, food, literature, and media. Worldly. Growing up, knowing different things was vital. When I was young, I didn't realize I was empowered. I thought I was weird. I felt embarrassed about learning things. It took me twenty years to overcome being the weird one.

FW: No, no, no. You should never apologize for being smart.

IC: When I went to college and studied psychology, I met individuals with knowledge in diverse areas. We learned from each other through discussions, shared insights, and talked about common interests. I formed friendships this way.

MW: Self-awareness is essential; intellect is crucial. Our son was also the "weird one." He was an outsider. He's a computer engineer, but he found his niche in computers in high school and surrounded himself with like-minded kids. He lives and works in Austin with people from around the world, from different races and backgrounds. We can appreciate the direction your parents insisted on when you were growing up. Good for them. Good for you.

IC: Don't misunderstand me. I like people but I prefer to be alone.

FW: We get it. No worries. Actually being introverted and managing a hospitality business speaks to your management skills and the fact that you started from the bottom and worked your way to the top management position is remarkable. How about other life experiences?

IC: I've traveled extensively, studied abroad, worked in various locations, and even owned a business. I have a fondness for exploring unconventional destinations and experiences. *I really like weird things.*

MW: There's that word again.

All: Laughter.

IC: One weird thing. When I graduated from hospitality school, I wanted to go to the North Pole and work in Finland. One year, I told my brother. He said okay, let's go. So we went to northern Finland.

FW: North Pole? Been there, done that. I lived in Greenland for one year.

IC: Oh my God. That's so interesting. You should write a book about that.

FW: That's another story for another time. So you love traveling?

IC: I love traveling, but I'm happy here.

MW: I've noticed consistency in your goals: travel, education, careers, mindset, and work ethic. Are there underlying reasons or influences you attribute this to?

IC: *Archery.*

FW: Archery?

IC: I studied and trained in archery as a teenager, between 15 and 19 years old. I got into it purely by accident. I had fallen and was unable to walk for weeks. So, my Physical Education teacher suggested I take up archery.

It turned out to be one of the best things in my life. I trained to become part of the Ecuadorian National team, but I injured my shoulder and had to stop. Because of my injury, I was sent to Guayaquil and met with the Olympic Committee to train to become an Olympic coach. I studied and trained for a couple of years, but unfortunately, the position was extended to someone else with ties to the Committee.

FW: Politics?

IC: I believe so. I loved archery. It taught me how to focus, be patient, concentrate, and practice introspection and grace, which are critical for me. I saw the results in my brother, who had struggles in school. When he started archery, he learned how to focus and became calmer. It helped him a lot in school, college, and work.

MW: You've excelled in roles where satisfaction is critical. Could you elaborate on how this influenced your decision to pursue a career in the hospitality industry and your future aspirations?

IC: I want to stay in the hospitality industry. I want to grow professionally, learn more, relearn German, and maybe live in Germany, but I want to remain in the industry.

MW: Everybody has memorable characters: strangers, heroes, and family members. They shape our beliefs, values, and memories. In many ways, they serve as mirrors reflecting aspects of ourselves and the world around us. They leave lasting impressions that significantly define who we are and aspire to become. Who are some of yours?

IC: Memorable, characters in my life? Well, my parents and my great-grandmother were remarkable. Also, my uncle. He's my mother's favorite brother. He's extraordinary but also very unconventional and very important in our household. He's very caring and helpful.

My great-grandmother was also a memorable person in my life. She took on the role of my dad's mother when his mother passed away when he was seven years old. She was 99 when she passed away. She was a storyteller and shared many stories of her childhood. She was amazing.

She remembered everybody working on the farm and caring for the houses. She remembered everything from her childhood: all the houses they owned, the harvests, what they cooked and drank, and all their parties. They were wealthy, and they would have huge parties during carnival. She remembers peacocks on the roofs destroying the roofs of the houses. The family estate provided a haven for us, the younger generation, to enjoy nature.

FW: I like to ask people we interview about their purpose in life. I realize it touches on the philosophical. How do you personally discover and cultivate it?

IC: My purpose is happiness; I want to cultivate joy within myself and spread it to others. Achieving this goal involves continual exploration and education. By traveling, I'll gain new experiences. This way, I hope to broaden my perspectives and understanding of different cultures and the world. Additionally, I want to explore deeper and more meaningful relationships with people from various backgrounds. It will enrich my life and provide opportunities for personal growth and development.

FW: Please provide insights into what makes Cuenca, Ecuador, unique.

IC: Cuenca offers the advantages of a larger city but in a more friendly setting. We have big-city amenities, but at the same time, you can keep local connections and relationships. It offers residents and visitors metropolitan conveniences but with the charm of a smaller town. Safety, rivers, and natural beauty add to our appeal, making it an attractive place for visitors. We have a broad food culture. Also, the climate in Cuenca remains pleasant year-round. Cuenca continues to grow and change. The influences of new people arriving from different countries add to our rich heritage. We take pride in our traditions and are eager to share our way of life with others.

FW: What impressions do international visitors typically hold of Cuenca within the hospitality industry?

IC: We have two types. Some have researched Cuenca and know what to expect, *while others think we live in trees.*

ALL: Laugher.

IC: There's this misconception that all South American countries are jungles. Maybe because part of the Amazon basin is in Ecuador. We've received inquiries from prospective guests about amenities such as hot water, showers, cars, telephone, internet, and all kinds of North American products from different countries. We need to inform them that we are a busy city center with a population of 750,000.

MW: So, what do you want people to know about Cuenca?

IC: I want them to know that Cuenca is a beautiful place, but it's not perfect. They should come prepared. Most importantly, they shouldn't expect everyone in Cuenca to speak English, and that living here without some basic Spanish language skills may be challenging.

FW: Do you have any regrets in your young life?

IC: None.

FW: None?

IC: None.

FW: Excellent. Why, I am not surprised. How about fears?

IC: My biggest fear is separating from my family. Because my boyfriend is an astrophysicist, I am still determining where we could live besides California. I wonder if he could live here and conduct his work remotely. Another fear is not having work-related opportunities.

FW: Job security. Understood.

Let's conclude the interview by discussing your passions and what makes you sad.

IC: Okay. I love my family, pets, traveling, job, food, learning, and experiencing new things. *I've learned that loving things is a good thing.* So, I try to love everything. What makes me sad is the situation in the world right now. Everyone seems to be suffering. Everyone needs a little love. What did that song say?

MW: What the world needs now is love?

FW: Jackie DeShannon song.

IC: What the world need now is love, sweet love.

FW: What a lovely way to end the interview. Thank you, Isabel, for being candid, open-minded, and willing to take on the challenge. It's been a pleasure talking with you, and we look forward to sharing your insights with our readers.

JONNATHAN PENA'S STORY

BORN AGAIN

"The truth is everyone is going to hurt you. You just have to find the ones that are worth hurting for."
-Bob Marley

I don't want you to think Jonnathan's story is sad. On the contrary, Jonathan's story is befitting of a Hollywood happy ending born of struggle. As a young man, he was deeply scarred by his parents' behavior and his father's childhood abandonment. And like many of us—who struggled through the indifference and callousness of fractured relationships, we somehow managed to endure, persevere, and prosper despite a painful and punishing twist of fate. Genetic roulette isn't fair. I get it. But it shouldn't determine life's opportunities, choices, and rewards of family, friendships, and culture.

Over time, he rediscovered the healing power of time, a rekindled love (Anabel Parro), and a passport to a new life—and is destined to live out his life with his long-lost love away from the parental world that abandoned him.

Photo credit, David Fajardo

Photo credit, Frederico Wilson

The more I reflected on Jonnathan's childhood anguish, the heart-wrenching song, *'Long, Long, Time'* written by Gary White and sung by Latino chanteuse Linda Ronstadt (a fellow Tucsonan), kept replaying in my head. It encapsulates Jonnathan's anguish and puts a spin on *unrequited love.*

Excerpts:

Love will abide; take things in stride.
Sounds like good advice, but there's no one at my side.
. . . Life's full of flaws; who knows the cause.
. . . Living in the memory of a love that never was.

It's a passionate, expressive cry about rejection and acknowledgment. The song resonates in some form because we're all vulnerable and rebuffed in our lifetimes. At a base level, it's a heartache that won't abate. We share the longing for loss and *feel* heartbreak and sorrow connecting us to others. It's a sad song about yearning for love, never getting love, and eventually coming to terms with the fact that sometimes we might have to face life alone and without support.

It's not in my nature to offer unsolicited counsel; however, sometimes, I feel obligated when circumstances decree it. I'm fond of Jonnathan. We both share[1] Latin American cultural heritage and bloodlines. And as 'genetic' brothers, we share a symbiotic connection forged and fueled in the cauldron of parental rejection.

I, like Jonnathan (thank goodness), chose to move on. Life is too short to spend an inordinate amount of time and reflection looking in the rearview mirror at what could have been and what we missed.

With all sincerity and candor, to Jonnathan and every child who has suffered the anguish hurled on them by misbehaving parents. Consider, you're not alone. Many parents misbehave badly. I realize its little consolation, but you probably weren't your parents' favorite child. But you probably knew that deep in your heart.

Much to their parents' consternation, siblings are keenly aware of which child among them was selected.

---

1. FW: [*I can relate to Jonnathan's plight and struggles at a core level. In early childhood, my old man chose to crow on the exploits of his namesake. Unfortunately, that would be me. He lived vicariously through my early accomplishments. Not fair, I grant you. But the old man's attention was compensatory; it offset his personal disappointments in life, evident to anyone seeking truth, not excuses or pretexts for self-pity. Not pretty, but there it is. When the primary accomplishments faded, so did he.*]

Parents choose one over others for many reasons, ranging from the sublime to the ridiculous, from deeply emotional, well-intentioned altruism to equally absurd vanity and superficiality. However predetermined, their choices invariably have far-reaching, often dire, and have long-lasting consequences.

To our dismay, parents would have you believe they're impartial arbitrators, sharing their love and attention equally with their children. Sadly, this isn't true. If you're honest with yourself, you know your parent's favorite child has benefited inordinately, and, as a result, you may need or may have already drawn on therapy to get over it.

Parents never were, nor will ever be, impartial, a curious and inexplicable Machiavellian peculiarity. It may be distressing to contemplate, but parents aware of their ability to create mini-fiefdoms are beguiled and predisposed to arbitrarily dispense power over their children. Exercising this authority irresponsibly, favoring one over others, leads to alienation.

All parents master the art of manipulation. They curry favor and wield influence in various forms with targeted praise and surgical precision, with stifled sighs of disappointment, snide asides, and even contemptuous disdain toward the unlucky. They are primarily responsible for their children's sociological and psychological integration into adulthood and civilized society.

In case we forgot, Mom and Dad, long before they decided to procreate and replicate imperfect little clones of themselves, had unresolved issues to contend with before they walked down the aisle. Those issues didn't magically disappear with matrimony. They took on a life of their own, in a new relationship and inevitably, with the introduction of children.

Throw various extenuating circumstances like job satisfaction, mobility, continuing education, money issues, and troubled marriage; children are no longer innocent bystanders. They become pawns and weapons, enlisted as confidants and allies, utilized to strengthen a feuding partner's position. This manipulative behavior creates dysfunction and splits relationships among family members.

Most siblings never recover, and they lead their lives damaged by their parent's partiality. The unfavored will forever envy the chosen one, and their childhood resentment is unforgotten. Conversely, the favored children will reap the rewards of privilege, resources, and entitlement extended to them by a biased parent. The results are a lifetime of grievances and disputes. Favored children continue throughout their lifetimes to reap the rewards bestowed on them, not surprisingly unearned.

My advice to Jonnathan is to accept a simple truth: that we, the children, are not at fault for the sins of our parents. We were never in control, nor were we capable of mapping out (initially) our destinies. Some of us escaped the baggage of our parents and managed to live productive and happy lives; others have struggled, and some of us, I fear, never will.

And, yes, I'm well aware that it's easy to blame parents for some of the shortcomings in our lives, but parents have a history, and marriage has a culture. And between the two, the children were not the adults in the room making the decisions.

Our parents both guided us and put us at risk. As

children, we do not question the wrongs of adults. *We suffer them.* To understand ourselves better, we must understand their motives and reasoning for misbehaving. Acknowledgment of anything less—dooms us forever to love a snapshot of our parents rather than a portrait and everlasting memory in our hearts.

So we must ask ourselves, am I the favored or unfavored child? Am I prepared to confront unfairness and privilege and move on with my life, no longer affected by parental partiality?

Nothing in early life affects us as profoundly as our parents do. They're our role models, and we learn to emulate them—sometimes, at our peril. They influence our relationships and shape the people that we become.

Better that, as adults, we escape their grip and construct our narratives by deconstructing their narratives about us. Only then can we extricate ourselves from their chosen world and move on to living independently.

"Life becomes easier when you learn to accept the apology you never got."
—Robert Brault (Author, "Reflections")

I'm happy to report that Jonnathan overcame the effects of his childhood abandonment and self-doubts.

He's successfully started **Sky Visa Consulting**, guiding foreigners in acquiring Ecuadorian visas and associated relocation matters. He can be contacted in Cuenca, Ecuador, at WhatsApp: 593 958735006. Email: skyvisasconsulting@gmail.com. Web: http://skyvisasconsulting.com.

Photo credit, Jonnathan Pena

JONNATHAN PENA
INTERVIEW

The interview with Jonnathan Pena occurred at "Raquel's Steakhouse" in Cuenca, Ecuador. Mary Wilson, a researcher and contributor, participated in the interview. The interview has been reconstructed from notes, audio text, translations, and recollections of conversations and edited to augment clarity.

[Abbreviations: JP: Jonnathan Pena, AB: Anabel Parro, FW: Frederico Wilson, MW: Mary Wilson]

Everybody is seated. Jonnathan is joined at the table by Anabel, his fiancé.
Our orders have been taken, and we've ordered wine for dinner.

FW: First of all, thank you for joining us in sharing your story. In a recorded interview, we invited you to share your culture, family background, memories, hopes, desires, and feelings about your Ecuadorian story. We intend to foster, shape, and share authentic Ecuadorian perspectives, a larger frame of reference for others worldwide to consider and contemplate. We believe every story has value; each is a unique human experience with context, characters, events, and opinions that interest someone if told and heard. And who better to tell multifaceted Latin American stories and viewpoints than the people who lived them? So, with that as a prologue, let's begin.

JP: I was born in Cuenca and am 34 years old. *My parents were never married.*

FW: Oookay! I wasn't expecting that. You caught me by surprise. But sure, we can start there.

JP: I retained my mother's name until I was three, when my biological father reappeared and gave me his name. He left shortly after, and I didn't see him again until I was ten years old, and he invited me to live in the

States. I was a kid and thought going to the States was a dream.

MW: Where in the United States?

JP: Connecticut. It wasn't what I expected. That's when I met my step-sister. Everything was strange, especially the weather. I remember the first time I saw snow. That was exciting! But after about three days, I said, "No more snow!"

All: Laugher.

JP: I never felt comfortable there because of my stepmother. She is Latina, but I think she is the second generation living in the country. She spoke Spanish but was mean, telling all my siblings to talk to me only in English. But after a while, I began to understand some English, and sometimes, she would say unkind things about me, thinking I didn't understand.

MW: But you did?

JP: Some. So I told my dad I didn't want to live there anymore. I felt alone in the United States.

FW: How old were you?

JP: I was twelve when I returned to Cuenca to live with my mom. That's when I met her (nodding to Anabel beside him). We were kids—innocent, just having fun—but I knew back then I felt something special about her. She was my best friend at the time, but then she moved to another neighborhood, and we lost touch. I also lost touch with my father until about ten years ago.

FW: Two pretty meaningful relationships, yes?

JP: (Nodding). I finished high school and returned to the States to work in New York with my uncle, who worked in construction. But my mom wanted me to come back to Cuenca to finish college. So, when I re-

turned, my mom pressured me to become an engineer. The problem was that I wanted to avoid becoming an engineer, so I skipped classes and dropped out—too much pressure from family and friends. I was lost. I needed to find out where I belonged.

Then I met a girl, and we got pregnant. So I have a son, Sebastian, and he and his mother live in the States. He's ten.

MW: And how is that working out?

JP: I see him often when his mother allows me to. There are a lot of rules.

FW: So, all this time, you've been undecided about what direction your life will take? What did you want to pursue career-wise?

JP: I returned to college and got a degree in business management. But my real passion has always been psychology. It requires an advanced degree and credits, so I'll have to return to school, but that's what I want to pursue.

MW: In the meantime, will you continue working at the law office?

[At the time of the interview, Jonathan worked at a law firm specializing in Expat visas and related legal matters. He now has his own firm.]

JP: Yes, throughout all this, I've been lucky to receive support from my family. My mom worked a lot, and my grandmother primarily raised me in the countryside.

FW: You're fortunate. I don't know what it is, but not all Latino parents, at least in the States, support their children equally. It's a mystery to me. Maybe it concerns the "American dream" myth they bought into over the years. Generation after generation, they prioritize consumerism over education and business. I understand that societal class comes into play. But it's been my experience that generally, poor and working-class Latino families are too demanding and too often unforgiving. They expect you to get out of the house—early. Expect you to go to work—early. And they expect you to go to school on your own and help them pay and support other children in the family—at the same time.

Forgive my rant. Wine frees the mind. It's been an impediment to young Latinos for generations. Latinos have been sold a bill of goods. They can find money to buy a shiny new pick-up truck or pay for their daughter's "quinceanera" or wedding, but paying for college—forget it. They've traded their children's prospects for *American lifestyle vanity*. I don't know what it's like here in Cuenca, but I suspect social media are bombarding young people with consumerism, and it's not much different. Latino values and priorities are twisted by Western society.

JP: Funny thing, but social media is how I reconnected with Anabel. I had just gotten my divorce papers and saw a familiar face on social media. It was Anabel.

MW: That's how he found you?

AP: (Smiling) Yes.

MW: Oh, that's great!

JP: I was looking at profiles and thought she looked familiar. I knew this girl, so I looked at her old profile pictures, and it was her. I sent a friend request and waited. She made me wait for weeks. Maybe she was in a relationship, had a boyfriend, or married. I began to wonder if she was my long-lost friend.

So, about that time, my grandmother returned from the States and invited all her old friends, including Anabel's father and mother, for a gathering. I started talking to them and asked them about Anabel and how she was doing. Anabel's mother says, "You can ask her yourself; she'll be here in a few minutes." I thought, "Is this happening?" I felt warm inside. I started talking and drinking with her dad, asking him questions about her until she entered. After several more drinks, I finally decided to speak to her. And the rest is fate.

[At this part of the interview, Anabel informs us in Spanish that she has an engineering degree and specializes in business administration. She also tells us that she has a one-year-old daughter named Samantha.]

MW: Destiny. What are the odds that 19 years later, you would find each other? What a beautiful story. Two children. Two S's, Sebastian and Samantha.

FW: Upon your return to the States, you must have immersed yourself in the language.

JP: Yes, I studied English, and my teacher was from the U.K. I started to speak with a British accent.

FW: You don't speak with any accent. You sound like an American. If you have English language skills in Cuenca, they are extremely valuable. I'm trying hard to recapture the Spanish I knew as a child, and Mary is taking Spanish classes. It's necessary to fit comfortably in the community.

JP: If you're here, you must accept that you must learn a little about the language and culture. If you don't want to, then why did you come?

FW: Exactly. Describe some of your encounters with expats in Cuenca.

JP: About five years ago, I met a couple. They were from Tennessee and had been living here for two years. The gentleman lost 85 pounds, and the lady lost 100 pounds because they changed their North American diet. They ate organic food and a lot of fresh fruit and vegetables. She cried; she was so happy about the weight loss and lifestyle change.

MW: Healthy and inexpensive.

FW: Let's play a word game. I will give you a word. Let me know the first thing that comes to mind.

JP: Word game?

FW: Yes. Philosophy.

JP: (Pausing) Tree roots.

FW: Elaborate.

JP: Roots are life's paths, all connected to the tree and extending to its branches. So, I have to decide which branch I should choose. These decisions come up all the time. Which path is my true self? Do outside factors and expectations influence me, or do I remain true to myself and take responsibility for my actions? You have to believe in your own mastery.

FW: Memories.

JP: The first time I saw my son. "I don't know who you'll become, but I can assure you I'll be there when you need me because my father wasn't." And the second best memory is when I saw Anabel again.

FW: What motivates you?

JP: When I was young, I made some terrible decisions. I was stupid. But now I know what I want. I'm in control, and I know how to get it.

FW: Regrets?

JP: I have some regrets, but I wouldn't be here right now if they hadn't happened. Everything I've overcome and achieved has brought me here, right? You learn from your mistakes. You grow up.

FW: Fear.

JP: Failure. I don't want to make the same mistakes I've made before. I don't want to fail my son when he needs me.

FW: Family matters are a common theme among everyone we've interviewed.

JP: It's more important than making money. There's nothing wrong with trying to make money, but getting together with the family, going out to the country over the weekend, relaxing, and sharing food and wine is more important.

FW: Happy. What makes you happy and sad?

JP: I have finally achieved the contentment I desire by finding joy in my life, maintaining a healthy relationship with Anabel, and hopefully sustaining it for the rest of my life. Instead of dwelling on past troubles, I can now look ahead with optimism. I recall the depths of my sadness when I reached a breaking point. Insecurity breeds sadness, draining one's energy. It's crucial to discover the person you're destined to become.

FW: What makes these interviews so interesting is the scope and depth of introspection and how people handle the obstacles they've had to overcome to reach a sense of serenity.

MW: Navigating personal and professional life is becoming more difficult for the younger generation, regardless of where they are. How are you handling it?

JP: *All young people should know where their tree roots are.* Education and knowing what you want out of life are equally important. Culture is essential, but it doesn't matter where you live. You will do well if you're rooted, have some morality, principles, and foundation, and have a family.

FW: That's very encouraging to hear. It's truly heartening to listen to your perspectives. With that, it seems fitting to draw our interview to a close. Your willingness to share has undoubtedly enriched our understanding. Thank you sincerely for offering glimpses into your journey. The adage 'the more we share, the more we learn' couldn't ring truer. It's been a truly enlightening conversation, and your insights have shed light on many important aspects. Your contributions are invaluable in adding authentic voices to *Stories from the Andes*. Thank you once again.

ANTONELLA MOLINA'S STORY

LIFE IS A TRAPEZE

You must learn to fly alone to find your place in the world.

In the grand circus of life, we often find ourselves perched on a precarious trapeze, swinging high above the crowd, navigating through a world full of unexpected twists and turns. This metaphorical trapeze represents our journey to discover our place in the world. This journey is seldom safe or predictable. Antonella's story is one such journey, a vivid reminder that sometimes, to truly find our place, we must learn to fly alone.

This young Ecuadorian woman embarked on her journey with an unyielding spirit, challenging the norms of a male-dominated world. Her life unfolded like a performance under the big top, filled with moments of grace and daring feats, all within a "no-safety-net" environment. It is a journey that exemplifies the courage required to defy societal expectations and break free from the confines of tradition.

The trapeze symbolizes pursuing one's dreams, soaring with grace and fearlessness. Like many young women, Antonella's journey was anything but straightforward.

Illustration credit, Catalina Carrasco

She had to confront the daunting reality of a world where opportunities and recognition were often denied to those who did not conform to traditional gender roles. In a society where the ground floor was a fleeting illusion for many young women, she knew that she had to find her own path in the circus of life.

Antonella's determination to break free from societal constraints echoes the struggle countless young women face worldwide, particularly in patriarchal societies like Ecuador. The trapeze of life, as she discovered, is not designed for those who fear heights or shy away from risks. It demands courage and resilience, qualities that Antonella possessed in abundance.

The trapeze also represents the constant pursuit of balance. Just as trapeze artists must maintain equilibrium as they swing, individuals like Antonella must find equilibrium in a world that often tilts against them. It's a delicate dance of navigating societal expectations, family pressures, and personal ambitions. Antonella refused to be weighed down by the expectations that sought to keep her grounded. Instead, she learned to soar, to find her own rhythm amid the chaos.

Antonella's journey serves as an inspiration for young women who dare to challenge the status quo. Her story illustrates the importance of learning to fly alone when the world seems determined to hold you back. She reminds us that life is full of uncertainties, but it is in those very uncertainties that we find our true selves. Just as trapeze artists must trust their abilities, Antonella learned to trust herself and her dreams.

In the grand circus of life, we must all become trapeze artists, learning to navigate the highs and lows, the twists and turns, and the moments of exhilaration and fear. Antonella's journey is a testament to the resilience of the human spirit, the capacity to rise above adversity, and the beauty of soaring freely through the limitless expanse of the sky.

Photo credit, Antonella Molina

As we watch Antonella gracefully swing through the air, we are reminded that life is a trapeze. We must learn to fly alone during this daring adventure to find our place in the world. It is a journey filled with challenges and uncertainties. Still, it is also a journey filled with the promise of self-discovery and fulfillment. Antonella's story reminds us that, just like her, we can defy gravity, break free from the safety net, and embrace the exhilarating journey of life with open arms.

ANTONELLA MOLINA

INTERVIEW

The interview with Antonella Molina occurred at "Café del Museo" Calle Paseo 3 Noviembre in Cuenca, Ecuador. Mary Wilson, a researcher and contributor, participated in the interview. The interview has been reconstructed from notes, audio text, translations, and recollections of conversations and edited to augment clarity.

[Abbreviations: AM: Antonella Molina, FW: Frederico Wilson, MW: Mary Wilson]

Mary and I are seated in the tranquil patio of the Café del Museo, a picturesque spot that offers a panoramic view of the Tomebamba River. This river, a lifeline for the City of Cuenca, merges into the Amazon River and eventually flows into the Atlantic Ocean. Antonella, a familiar face from our previous visit to Cuenca, approaches our table as we prepare to order lunch. In a heartwarming display of Ecuadorian custom, she warmly embraces and kisses Mary on the cheek, a gesture that speaks volumes about their genuine connection.

FW: (Hugging her) Welcome. Nice to see you again.

AM: Nice to see you. Thank you for the invitation. I'm a little nervous.

FW: (Handing her a printout of questions we would cover) No problem. Relax. Let's order some wine and give you time to review some of the talking points. This interview aims to delve into how Ecuadorian and, specifically, Cuenca culture, as seen through your unique lens, has shaped your perspectives on life. Your insights, as a local, are invaluable in our quest to provide a comprehensive understanding of the local culture. There are a lot of stories written by expats for expats, and we wondered why nobody took the approach of interviewing locals to understand local culture better.

AM: (Nodding) Culture is everything.

[At this point, our waiter takes our orders, giving Antonella additional time to review the printout.]

FW: Listo para ir? (Ready to go?)

AM: Lista. (Ready)

FW: How old are you?

AM: I just turned 24.

MW: And where is your family from?

AM: My parents come from two different small towns outside Cuenca. They met here at my Aunt's wedding in Cuenca. It was fate, but the family relations and connections became broken and complicated through tragic events over the years. My grandfather on my mother's side initially owned land, built houses, and owned businesses outside Cuenca. But when my mother was 20 years old, my grandmother got sick and died. My mother tells me that it was a sorrowful time. My grandmother was the matriarch of the family. My grandfather was lost because my grandmother handled a lot of the business. Grieving, he sold everything and moved to Spain—first to Madrid and then to a smaller town. So he's lived in Spain for over thirty years, and all during that time, he helped support family members in Cuenca.

FW: So when did you meet him?

AM: When I was about 12 years old I went to New Jersey with my family. I met him on a road trip from there to Miami. I had a chance to talk to him all along the way. We would stop at different places and take pictures. We bonded on that trip. Many years later he remarried in Spain and had children. Anyways I got a chance to fulfill a childhood dream and went to Disneyland. It was terrific, a great experience.

MW: Speaking of childhood, do you envision having children in the future, if you don't mind me asking? Considering your upbringing in Ecuador with your family, do you think it might influence your approach to parenting?

AM: I would love to have kids in the future. When they're young, it's vital to introduce them to nature. Some of my best memories are spent in the countryside and nature. I am so grateful that my parents felt their children needed to spend time outdoors. When you're a child, you're just living your life unless you have to work when you're a kid. That's so sad. The most important thing I can offer my children is a healthy childhood. I couldn't have asked for anything better than my family.

FW: Everybody we've met is family-oriented. That's not necessarily the case in the States. They live in a bubble. My childhood was similar to yours. We spent a lot of time outdoors playing with siblings and cousins. When I was a kid, it was a tradition to picnic at sandy riverbeds outside of town every Easter. We would play baseball, one family against the other.

AM: We experienced things like that many years before, but now, not so much. Life gets too busy. You have to decide to spend time with your family. If you go to my grandmother's house every day, it's full. There's always somebody there. Ever since I can remember, I could sit and talk to them on Sundays.

It's a day I can touch them.

Now that I'm working on Sundays, I have decided to visit with them, even if I'm late for lunch. One of my biggest fears is losing time with them.

Unfortunately, this year I haven't been able to go *every* Sunday. They feel bad for me. They are very protective. "Are you eating" they ask. "Do you have an umbrella?" Do you want us to pick you up?" My father is not like that. He's more balanced. He knows I have to do things on my own. My father thinks my mother is too protective. She's like that with all the children. If I work late and say I'm hungry she wants to make me something. I sometimes have to remind her that I'm 24.

ALL: [Laugher.]

MW: You're college educated. Speak to us a little about your professional aspirations.

AM: I never thought business administration could be an option. My father was an engineer, so that career path was always on my mind. So I checked into it, but the classes had already started. For a while, I didn't know what to do. I was lost. My friends were already studying, and I felt pressure to make a career decision. I didn't do anything for about six months and realized that I like numbers. I love this, I thought. Why don't I try to study business administration? My college thesis was in business administration, which eventually led me into the hospitality industry. I would love to work for a company with upward mobility that would allow me to grow in human resources and general business management.

MW: As we shift our focus to your early years and family background, could you share some insights on that? How has your family shaped who you are today?

AM: Everything is connected to the family. I had a beautiful childhood and very fond memories of it. I point out this because many people do not have happy childhoods. I am very fortunate I haven't had too many bad moments. However, when my grandfather died, it was tough for my father. How his loss affected him touched

me deeply. It was a very sad moment in my life—a defining moment in my life. I also have an extraordinary relationship with my mother. Although we have different personalities, *our relationship is gold.*

FW: The passing of family and friends is a significant touchstone in our lives. Let's talk about happier times.

AM: Graduating, of course. And I want to own my own business in the future. That will make me very happy. Once you envision it, it's just a matter of time.

FW: A worthy goal. And on the personal side of things?

AM: It sounds cliché, but I want to be happy. I know people with a lot of money who could be happier. It could be because they need a base or a support group.

MW: Well, you're off to a good start. A solid foundation. Building blocks. An education, a supporting family, aspirations, and a healthy lifestyle.

FW: And curiosity. Curiosity will open doors for you. Always keep an open mind.

AM: That's what I try to do. I experiment and try new things.

MW: I'm interested in your general outlook on life. I understand you want to pursue a business career and open a business. On the personal side, what motivates you? What do you think about when you wake up in the morning?

AM: Like my purpose? Bloody, wake up!

All: [Laughter!]

AM: When I wake, I think, what am I doing today? What am I going to accomplish today? What am I going to argue about with my Mom? How can I be a better person? There are things we can continually improve. And how will I do it in a way that makes me happy? Then I pet my dog.

FW: (Smiling) Then you pet your dog? Oh, good one. That's an excellent beginning to each day.

FW: Do you have any regrets at this early stage of your life?

AM: My father always said we shouldn't have any regrets because we can't change what we've done. The best thing is to learn what we could have done better. So, no. No regrets.

FW: Quickfire. Trust me when I say I'm asking you this openly and thoughtfully. What do you think about when I say the following words? Please give me the first thing that comes to mind: fear.

AM: (Confidently nodding no) No fear.

FW: Wow!

FW: Love.

AM: It's the most important thing. It's what moves me.

FW: Future.

AM: I dream about it often. No limits. Belief in myself.

FW: Sadness.

AM: Oh, bad memories. I cry a lot. If I see a sad movie, I cry.

FW: Happiness.

AM: Generally, love. Family, friends, and music make me happy. Good weather, even rain, makes me happy.

FW: Good sport. Thank you for playing along.

FW: Let's talk about Cuenca. What makes Cuenca unique?

AM: Culture. Specifically, how people from Cuenca interact with one another. Even if we don't know each other, we're kind to each other (Smiling) Okay, almost everybody is friendly to one another. And we extend that to people that are from somewhere else. Our culture makes them feel welcome.

FW: What do you think about people from the North?

AM: They need to understand people from the South. They need help understanding South America and Latin American culture in general. Money is important to us, but family is more important to us. Nature and architecture are essential to us.

FW: When we embarked on this project, we made a concerted effort to interview young people from the region to gain their perspectives. I can't thank you enough for participating in this project and sharing your insights.

AM: (Grinning) You're welcome. I'm not nervous anymore.

POSTSCRIPT

I'm happy to report Antonella has successfully transitioned from the hospitality industry to Medical Operational Management. We wish her every success.

MATEO JIMENEZ'S STORY

REINVENTION

Sometimes, life is an odyssey of unexpected circumstances.

Raised amidst a backdrop of familial turbulence, nurtured by the guiding hands of his grandparents, Mateo's story is one of broken dreams, unanticipated hurdles, and, ultimately, one triumphant redefinition and purpose.

Born into a fragmented family, Mateo was primarily raised by his loving grandparents, who instilled in him values of compassion and determination. He dreamed of becoming a professional football goalie as a young, athletic man. With football being the lifeblood of Ecuadorian culture, Mateo believed his ticket to escape the adversities that loomed over his broken home lay between the goalposts. His aspirations, however, were shattered when he sustained a permanent shoulder injury, demolishing his dreams.

To complicate his circumstances further, life presented Mateo with an unexpected twist when his girlfriend became pregnant. Confronted with the impending responsibilities of becoming a father, Mateo experienced

Illustration credit, Catalina Carrasco

a profound realization that his life was on the verge of undergoing a significant transformation. Confronted by the formidable prospect of supporting a family, he recognized the necessity for change.

Having his ambitions dashed by a physical setback and realizing the upcoming demands of a new family, Mateo made a conscious pivot to the tranquility of nature and the reflective practice of meditation. They enabled him to navigate the turbulence of these thoughts, dreams, and fears. The serene landscapes of Cuenca, interspersed with its lush green mountains, mirrored his transformation—a new path from the rubble of his shattered dreams.

He embarked on *reinventing himself.* He turned his affection for his city into a viable career—tourism. With its cobblestone streets, majestic churches, and captivating landscapes, Cuenca offered the perfect canvas for his newfound interest.

He realized that he had to learn English and gain a college degree in tourism, quintessential skills in a country flourishing with tourism yet still grappling with language barriers. With this newfound direction, Mateo committed to providing for his newborn child, Luciana, and supporting his wife, Nicole. He found strength in his love for them and the promise of a brighter future he could envision.

In the process, he learned that objectives aren't static but are fluid and can be reshaped. His initial desire to become a professional football player might have been unattainable. Still, his visions of providing a better life for his family were within his grasp.

The pursuit of this new path took work. Between juggling the pressures of becoming a new father, hus-

Photograph credit, Mateo Jimenez

band, and full-time student, Mateo often found himself on the brink of exhaustion. However, his experiences had hardened him, and he persisted by drawing strength from his meditation.

What's to be gained from Mateo's story? There are lessons to learn: the inherent ability to reinvent oneself and the courage to dream anew. His resilience in the face of hardship, the audacity to shatter the shackles of a predetermined future, and his continual commitment to learning and growing are inspirational.

Above all, Mateo adapted. His journey reminds us that life is an ebb and flow of circumstances, and our ability to swim with the current defines our survival. Life is like that sometimes. Random, sudden, unforeseen, unpredictable. Sometimes, life simply gets in the way. Through the unexpected changes that life thrust upon him, he learned that dreams may shatter, but that does not constrain new possibilities. On the contrary, it becomes an opportunity to mold new dreams from the fragments of the old.

Resilience is a common theme throughout Ecuador. Life is hard. Opportunities are few. Mateo's grandparents taught him to stand firm in the face of adversity. His injury taught him the power of acceptance, to let go of what was, to make room for what could be. His girlfriend's unexpected pregnancy showed him the essence of responsibility, and the birth of his child brought him face-to-face with the meaning of unconditional love. It serves as a reminder that life is an ever-evolving narrative characterized by unexpected twists and turns. But even amidst chaos and uncertainty, finding a new path of stability, growth, and happiness is possible.

It's common for people's aspirations and plans to change due to unforeseen circumstances such as injury, family responsibilities, or other life events. But it takes a special kind of person to rise above misfortune. Mateo is a testament to the human spirit's ability to rise above adversities.

Broken dreams can indeed be the foundation
of new and fulfilling ones.
It's about turning setbacks into stepping stones.

MATEO JIMENEZ

INTERVIEW

The interview with Mateo Jimenez took place at "Jodaco's Belgian Bistro" in San Sebastian Plaza, Cuenca, Ecuador, where both English and Spanish were spoken. Mary Wilson, a researcher and contributor, and Leonardo Duran, a translator, participated in the interview. The text has been reconstructed and edited to augment consistency and clarity.

[Abbreviations: MJ: Mateo Jimenez, FW: Frederico Wilson, MW: Mary Wilson, LD: Leonardo Duran.]

FW: Thank you for joining us today. We're eager to hear your unique story about life in Cuenca. Please share your story and how it has shaped your identity.

MJ: I am 25 years old. I pursued a tourism license at the Universidad Del Azuay, and this year, I became a father.

FW: Wow. That's a lot of ground to cover. Let's start at the beginning.

MJ: I was born into a family with young parents who were my age at the time. Despite being the second child, I grew up in a busy household with three siblings. My childhood, however, was spent mainly with my grandparents, both on my parents' and mother's side. They played significant roles in my upbringing.

I never experienced material needs, but I did endure a separation from my parents. So, whether I desire it or not, it leaves its mark. It shapes your life. As a consequence, I find myself much closer to my grandparents and siblings than to my parents. I also have a younger sister and an older brother.

MW: Tell us a little about your early childhood.

MJ: I have been playing soccer since I was very little. Football has always been a passion of mine. I began coaching soccer, initially as a goalkeeper. Later, I focused on soccer training, driven by my childhood dream of becoming a professional soccer player, a dream shared by many children here in Ecuador. Eventually, I started training at Club Deportivo Cuenca, the city team.

MW: And your early childhood schooling?

MJ: I attended the German School in Cuenca, a respectable institution offering kindergarten through seventh-grade education. Following that, I transitioned to Colegio Santa Ana. During my time at primary school, I was shy, but upon switching to a new environment, I transformed. At Colegio Santa Ana, I had greater freedom to express my thoughts and feelings. I learned many values that the German Colegio Alemán lacked. Specifically, they instilled in me a deep appreciation for nature. I was taught the importance of observing nature, gaining self-knowledge, and practicing self-care through meditation. These principles are essential for understanding oneself as a human being and recognizing the importance of nurturing both the body and the mind. This lesson stayed with me, and I found it very valuable. Once a month, we went on nature walks to different mountains or waterfalls.

I made friends that I know will last me a lifetime. What brought us all together was learning to laugh at ourselves during that stage of school when we had a lot of insecurities and problems. That unites us today and is a significant part of my life. That's why I enjoyed school so much.

FW: So early on, you dreamed of becoming a soccer player. What happened to the dream?

MJ: At the age of 15, I suffered a shoulder injury that continues to bother me to this day, forcing me to halt my quest of the sport. Although I attempted to play despite the pain, it was too much of a struggle. The injury occurred during a training session when I landed awkwardly on my shoulder, causing damage to a membrane surrounding the bone. It required surgery.

MW: So the dream was crushed. How did you cope? How did you handle the disappointment?

MJ: I'm still in school, continuing to live an adolescent life—you know, doing all the things people my age do, normal experimentation, and such. I'm OK with my situation and was looking forward to graduating, yet I was uncertain about my future path. With plenty of free time, I was drawn to meditation, which had always intrigued me. Searching online, I came across a forty-two-day course grounded in Buddhist principles.

I began this program intending to meditate, but I abandoned it after just 20 days. What's interesting is that it eventually became linked with everything else. At the time, I was 18 years old and fresh out of school. The appeal of a life filled with parties and youthful pursuits seemed unstoppable.

The program consisted of refraining from pornography, intoxicants, tobacco, alcohol, or drugs, and controlling sexual behavior. It occurred that this is quite a challenge for an 18-year-old. I need more life experience to grasp it fully.

Hormones were battling against Buddhist teachings.

All: [Laughter]

FW: Let me guess who won.

ALL: [Laughter]

FW: So, at this point, you're experimenting and exploring the direction your life will take.

MJ: Around this time, my uncle became a tour guide. Despite being my father's brother, our relationship wasn't close. My interactions with his family were limited but friendly. One day, during a conversation, he asked me about my goals. I expressed interest in following in his footsteps, leading me to study tourism.

Beyond academics, it was a time for exploration and new experiences. While attending University, I was free of major responsibilities. The only obstacle in my path was financial considerations, leading me to join my uncle and grandfather in their endeavors.

I had some unforgettable experiences at the University due to the cyclical nature of tourism, which occurs every six months. We took a technical tour spanning the country, starting from the coastal mountains and going eastward. We aimed to visit all 24 provinces and successfully achieved that goal. These trips offered numerous unforgettable moments and experiences.

After graduating, I found myself at a crossroads, wondering which direction to go, whether in guiding, hospitality, planning, or project development. To avoid stress, I decided to explore each option. I experimented with tour guiding through two infrequent jobs and discovered a fondness for it. However, the inconsistent nature of the work did not provide steady employment.

MW: Is this when you transitioned to the hospitality industry?

MJ: Yes, I began working in the industry. During this time, the University's curriculum changed, which required me to take additional classes and credits to graduate. I recently completed the courses, passed the exams, and will finish my thesis this month.

FW: Congratulations!

MJ: I enjoyed having a job and no longer have to study. I stopped going out with my friends and partying and started exercising again. I remembered the meditation program I had left when I was eighteen. At first, it was challenging. I had to cut my bad habits. I stopped smoking and drinking. After the second week, I noticed that I was much calmer. My mind no longer wandered. It was easier to focus. I started to like these small changes. Then, by the 24th day, I experienced the most beautiful day. I went to work and prepared for that day's meditation. I didn't expect anything different, but I was incredibly calm. I felt something I had never felt in my life, not with drugs and alcohol, not with anyone. I felt so at peace I took a photo of myself.

I cried. It had been a long time since I had cried.

MW: You had an epiphany—a realization of meaning and clarity. You experienced a personal understanding through meditation.

MJ: I continued and finished the program with my coach, who was from Albania.

FW: And do you still practice the steps in the program?

MJ: I am more disciplined but young and human after all—I occasionally have a beer.

ALL: [Laughter]

FW: In the beginning, you mentioned you became a father.

MJ: Until October last year, I was unaware I would become a father. My partner and I had been dating for six years. However, it was quite a shock when we discovered we would be parents. Parenthood wasn't something we had planned for at our age. Nevertheless, we embraced this new chapter in our lives.

Right from the start, we prioritized understanding the entire process. It was a reflective experience. We attended all the necessary check-ups, making sure that everything was progressing smoothly. Although we were familiar with how life develops up to the point of hearing the heartbeat, we were still uncertain whether we were ready to continue creating another human being.

Both of us lived with our parents. I resided with my mother while she stayed with her two parents. Neither parents were aware of the situation. There's a lot of pressure thinking about the worst-case scenarios. We didn't know with any certainty how our parents would react.

One day, I reached a breaking point; it was the strangest sensation. We told our parents on December 18th; it marked the best day of my life. After that peculiar moment, things settled down. Eventually, we decided to move in together, presenting another challenge: living as a couple required merging our backgrounds, customs, and habits. Isn't it all quite complicated?

FW: Very challenging. All young parents go through it.

MJ: I had to adapt to all of this. I felt like I didn't have enough money to support a baby and provide her with everything I wanted to offer. I wasn't earning enough. Consequently, I began searching for work despite the economic austerity. I ended up taking on two jobs, and the work was tough.

I found myself with no time for exercise or anything else besides work. Adding to the stress, my girlfriend experienced a complicated pregnancy, putting her at risk of miscarriage. I had to prioritize caring for her alongside my job. Consequently, I left my current position and began searching for new opportunities. During this search, I came across a job opportunity at this hotel, which seemed promising. Although the salary was lower, the schedule was better, allowing me to return to work for my uncle and grandfather.

MW: Now that you're a father and employed, I assume your life goals have changed.

MJ: I want to avoid my parents' mistakes and follow my grandparents' example. My purpose now is my baby and my love for my girlfriend.

MW: Mateo, life is unpredictable and complex, wouldn't you agree? The hurdles we must overcome disrupt our plans and aspirations and offer new opportunities for growth and self-discovery.

FW: You've embraced these challenges responsibly. You'll emerge stronger and wiser from these experiences.

FW: Finally, given your experience in the hospitality business, what are your thoughts about expats in Cuenca?

MJ: When arriving, most need help understanding Cuenca or South America. They thought Ecuador was a tropical country with jungles and beaches. But after a while, they think of Cuenca as a paradise because of its tranquility. That's a good thing because it gives the city a favorable identity.

FW: With that observation, I'd like to thank you for sitting down and giving us an insight into your life and Cuenca. It's been a pleasure meeting you and listening to your story.

CUENCA SNAPSHOTS

- Green Spaces
- Modern Condominiums
- Riverwalk
- Panoramic Views
- Hospital Del Rio Guardians

- Culinary Options
- Plazas
- Botanical Garden
- Historic Catedral
- Panama Hats

Maximillian and Max (the dog), Mary Wilson—Photo credit, Frederico Wilson

Puerta del Sol bridge connecting 3 Noviembre y Calle 12 Abril

Cantina La Unica—El Centro

Condos—Calle 12 Abril

Edificio—Puerta del Sol

Entrance—Kolo Restaurant & Bakery

Hallway—Mansion Matilde Restaurant—Corner of Parque Calderon

Illuminated domes—Catedral de la Inmaculada Concepcion

Jardin Botanico de Cuenca

Kolo Restaurant Mezzanine

Negroni Rooftop Restaurant

Parque Calderon

Plaza de las Flores—El Centro

Puerta del Sol—Tomebamba River Walk

San Sebastian Plaza

Seminario San Luis—Restaurants & Cultural Plaza

Solarium Country Estate

Terrace view—Cajas National Park at a distance

Tiestos Restaurant

Panama Hats, Toquilleras Artesanales, SigSig, Ecuador

EPILOGUE

STORIES ARE THE STRANDS THAT BIND US.

The thing about writing a book is that it grants you the intellectual and emotional freedom to explore and express an opinion on multiple topics. The challenge in compiling the material for this book was harnessing and comparing my journey, my story, my way of life, and my set of attitudes to those different from mine.

While conducting interviews, did I believe the inquiry and responses to be genuine, or was I being deceived? Did the interviewees pledge fidelity to their character, nature, and agency? I realized, of course, that experiences and environment influence attitudes, conduct, and worldview. But still. The deliberations lingered—a verdict in need of acquittal or sentencing.

After taking inventory of preconceptions, I've concluded that to embrace different cultures, one needs to travel and examine individual strengths and weaknesses directly, in person. *So, yes, the interviews were genuine—anchored to conscience and self-awareness.*

I discovered thinking we're "better" because we happen to be born into a specific country or belong to particular groups, i.e., religion, caste, race, ethnicity, gender—is delusional. We accommodate this failing and lapses in judgment because it's easy; it doesn't require critical thinking, self-reflection, and effort—merely rationalization. Consequences be damned, we reason.

> *"The unexamined life is not worth living."*
> —*Socrates*

Irrational behavior, yet another human ineptitude and predisposition, is part of human nature; I get it. But if everybody thought the same way, we'd never reach what I believe deep in our collective consciousness we all crave—an accepting, harmonious, peaceful, community, and *objective truth.*

I discovered that regardless of country, cultures worldwide serve to buffer, protect, and empower to equal degrees. On the other hand, it also unwittingly sacrifices individual expression and sovereignty at the altar of the established order.

On the surface, my suppositions may seem overly simplistic, given the complexities of other life experiences widely different from mine. And that's to be expected. However, all of life's intricacies eventually reach a common juncture—that moment and point when we contextualize our views of one another. Life's easy if we get out of our way. All we have to do is listen. It's up to us. The world is ours to change.

To summarize, allow me to contextualize my view of a people and culture—in the brief encounter I experienced alongside a pastoral winding road outside of Cuenca, Ecuador—with the "Orchid Woman."

ORCHID WOMAN

Ecuador boasts a rich tapestry of orchid biodiversity, boasting more than 4200 species of these exquisite flowers. My wife, Mary, and I visited Ecuagenera, nestled in the Ecuadorian Highlands near Cuenca in the Azuay Province.

Photo credit, Frederico Wilson

Photo credit, Frederico Wilson

As we wandered through the nursery, marveling at the stunning variety of orchids, an elderly, distinguished, and utterly charming Ecuadorian woman approached me and gently tapped my shoulder. She asked if I spoke Spanish, and I replied, "Yes, but not fluently." Her amusement was evident as she flashed a wry smile and delicately took hold of my arm, sharing with me a whispered revelation:

"¿Sabías que cuando Dios se aburría y quería jugar, creaba las orquídeas?"

["Did you know that when God grew weary and sought amusement, he created orchids?"]

Her choice to engage with me in that moment remains a mystery, but her touch and soft-spoken words stirred something deep inside me. I was rendered speechless by the profound statement; my heart moved beyond words. With a knowing eyebrow raised, she acknowledged my smile, and then, with unhurried grace, she ambled over to a middle-aged woman who awaited her, ready to escort her to their waiting car.

Looking back, I regret not seizing the opportunity to request an interview for my book. However, in hindsight, she possessed an innate understanding that I would carry her aphorism with me and share it with the world.

To the mysterious and enigmatic "Orchid Woman," I extend my heartfelt gratitude. Your wisdom will forever echo in my heart and, perhaps, resonate with those who hear it.

From your lips to God's ears.

AUTHOR PAGE

Frederico Lara Wilson, a former global Telecommunications and Fluid Power business owner and corporate executive, is an essayist and the author of the "Escaping Culture" series of books. As a multiethnic Latino, White, and Pascua Yaqui Indian, he explores societal issues through a multicultural lens. His writings characterize the richness and liberation of culture and how honest introspection and accountability have the power to craft, enhance, and control our lives and our future. He lives, works, and writes in metropolitan Seattle, Washington.

Photo credit, Mary Wilson

BOOKS—NON FICTION— AVAILABLE ON AMAZON

Escaping Culture—Finding Your Place in the World (Identity, Recollections, Empowerment)
Escaping Culture—The Reckoning (Social Commentary, Parody, Images)
Escaping Culture—Stories from the Andes (Through the Eyes of Ecuadorians)

2025
Escaping Culture—Renewal and Regeneration

CONTACT INFORMATION

Email: escapingculture@gmail.com

https://www.escapingculture.com
Facebook: https://www.facebook.com/EscapingCulture

CONTRIBUTORS

Mary Ellen Wilson
Researcher, Interviewer, Editor

Leonardo Duran
Logistics, Translator, Interviewer

CONTACT PAGE INFORMATION

CATALINA CARRASCO

Website: www.catalinacarrasco.com
Cellular: (593) 0992149751
Art Workshop: Cuenca / Vilcabamba – Ecuador
Facebook: https://www.facebook.com/elartedecata?mibextid=LQQJ4d
Stanford University • Pacific Art League • Visual Arts • Art Direction
Fine Arts • Illustration • Restoration

Born in Cuenca, Ecuador, Catalina has developed in different geographical parameters and cultural spaces, in intimate contact with painting, music, literature, photography and performing arts. Her love for art, together with a playful approach to the free act of creating that she calls "guiding star" make her work an experimental compendium. She considers that her relationship with creativity is an act of persistent surprise in a yearning for observation and listening. She has stated that most of her work subsists as an arrow that emerges from an invisible bow. Each image, each assembly and installation is the result of a matter of courage without a traced destination. A continuity of impermanence, an intimate effort to enter into a trance and cross the borders through that untouchable echo: Art.

Nacida en Cuenca, Ecuador, Catalina se ha desenvuelto en diversos parámetros geográficos y espacios culturales, en un contacto íntimo con la pintura, la música, la literatura, la fotografía y las artes escénicas. Su amor por el arte, junto con un enfoque lúdico hacia el acto libre de crear que ella llama "estrella guía" hace de su trabajo un compendio experimental. Considera que su relación con la creatividad es un acto de persistente sorpresa en un anhelo de observación y escucha. Ella ha declarado que la mayor parte de su trabajo subsiste como una flecha que se desprende de un arco invisible. Cada imagen, cada ensamblaje e instalación es el resultado de una cuestión de coraje sin un destino trazado. Una continuidad de impermanencia, un esfuerzo íntimo por ingresar en un trance y cruzar las fronteras, a través de ese eco Intocable: El Arte.

DAVID FAJARDO TORRES.

Personal contact:
E-mail: David.ft.18@hotmail.com.
WhatsApp: +593 987075453.
Contact for donations: Yasunidos social organization.
E-mail: guapondeligyasunidos@gmail.com
WhatsApp: +593 987075453.

TARIQ SAFIEH (PHOTOGRAPHY)

Email: safieh.tariq@gmail.com
Website: https://www.tariqsafieh.com

JONNATHAN PEÑA (VISAS)

Personal email: jonnathan.penat@gmail.com
Business email: skyvisasconsulting@gmail.com
Phone: 0958735006 +593 95 873 5006
Web: https://skyvisasconsulting.com
Visas, Immigration Services, Translation Services, Home Search Assistance

DRA. LORENA ESTEFANÍA VINTIMILLA MARTÍNEZ

Website: quick therapy IV
lorenavintimillam-15@hotmail.com
+593984682624
Business address: Hospital José Carrasco Arteaga Cuenca-Ecuador
Also providing services to all expats and local U.S.Veterans

LEONARDO DURÁN

Technology Consultant, Culture Ambassador
WhatsApp: +593983522685
Email: techguyec2020@gmail.com

MATEO JIMENEZ

LICENSED Tour Guide
Email: mateo_jimenez97@hotmail.com
Phone: +593 98 774 5367

JOSE IBANEZ/CALVO & CO.

Calvo & Co. Restaurant
Luis Moreno Mora y Cornelio Merchan
Cuenca, Ecuador
+593 95 879 3723

JUAN CARLOS SOLANO/TIESTOS RESTAURANT

Juan Jaramillo 4-89 y Mariano Cueva
Cuenca, Ecuador
www.tiestoscaferestaurant.com
+593 7-283-5310

ISABEL CASAJOANA/GRAND COLOMBIA SUITES

Gran Colombia Suites
Gran Colombia y Luis Cordero esquina (corner)
www.grancolombiasuites.com
Info@grancolombiasuites.com
072829862 593 72829862

CARLOS A. IGLESIAS CABRERA

Ciglesias09@hotmail.com
WhatsApp: 0999847794

CARLOS LARA

Guia Nacional de Turismo
Email: green_explorador@yahoo.com
WhatsApp: +593999797394

RESOURCES

(Abbreviated – Contact Facebook Group listings for additional resource information)

MEDICAL

Hospital Del Rio
WhatsApp: 099-5698637
Email: admisiones.caja@hospirio.com.ec
Address: Av. 24 de Mayo y Av. de las Americas

Find Health in Ecuador Dental Clinic
Email Address: info@findhealthinecuador.com
WhatsApp: 098-392-9606 / 07-410-8745 (Ecuador)
   1-941-227-0144 (USA)
Address: Edificio Medimagen (Second Floor) AV.
   Pumpaungo & Av. Paseo de los Canaris
Cuenca, Ecuador 010105
Websites: www.findhealthinecuador.com
   www.dentaltourismecuador.com

Blue Box Insurance (Medical)
Cuenca – Manta - Bahia de Caraquez
Website: www.blueboxinsurance.com
Address: Cuenca - Edif. Monte Carlo Oficina 001
Manta - Plaza Aventura Segundo Piso - Vía Barbasquillo

Eloy Alfaro Pharmacy
WhatsApp: 099-563-2090
Email: rebenavidezj@gmail.com
Address: Ordoñez Lasso Avenue and Alamos
   (next to the gas station)

Medical Facilitator and Personal Assistant
Diana Vera
WhatsApp: 099-174-4740
Email: diana81@vera@gmail.com

HOSPITALITY

Four Points by Sheraton Cuenca Hotel
Location: Next to Mall Del Rio
Av. Circunvalacion Sur y Ave. Felipe II
+593 7-602-2000

Hotel Victoria
WhatsApp: 099-309-9131
Email: Infor@hotelvictoriaecuador.com
Address: Calle Larga 6-93 y Presidente Borrero

Gran Colombia Suites
WhatsApp: 098 149 4693
Website: https://grancolombiasuites.com
Address: C. Luis Cordero 10-13 Cuenca, Ecuador

EB Hotel (Eurobuilding)
Address. Calle 24 de Septiembre S2-389 Tababela,
    Quito, Ecuador
Tele: +593 2 394 1020 +593 9 8363 0577
reservasquito@ebhotels.com
www.ebhotels.com/quito

RESTAURANTS

Solana Bistro
Av. de Solana y 12 de Abril
+593 99 109-9185
Facebook.com/solanobistroEC/
Email: solanobistro@gmail.com

La Yunta
WhatsApp: 098-945-6551
Address: Av. Primero de Mayo

Hostal Yakumama/Bistro Yaku
Address: 5-66, C. Luis Cordero 5-66 y Honorato
    Vasquez
+593 7-283 4353

Jodoco Belgian Bistro
WhatsApp: 097-909-3186
Address: Calle San Sebastian y Mariscal Sucre

Cafe del Museo
WhatsApp: 099-378-0721
Menu: https://sociedadgourmet.ec
Address: Calle Paseo Tres de Noviembre

Café Del Parque Restaurant & Cocktail Bar
Address: Av. del Estadio
Tele: +593 97-901-7471

La Cigale Restaurant & Hostal

Address: Honorato Vasquez 7-80 y Luis Cordero

Tele: +593 7-283-5308

Artesana Family Bakery

Food/Bakery Delivery

+593 99 879 2985

Sabatino's Garden Restaurant

Sabatinos.restaurante@gmail.com

+593 98 704 2538

Hosts Gran Feria (vendor fair) on most Saturdays

Address: Roberto Aguilar y 3 Noviembre

(one block west of Otorongo Plaza)

TRANSPORTATION SERVICES

Tranvia de Cuenca (Tram Line)

Purchase rechargeable transit cards at the ETAPA Office

Grand Colombia y Tarqui

https://Tranvia.cuenca.gob.ec/#/uso

Taxi
Eli Andres (Bilingual)

+593 99 648 3972

Cuenca

Also available for day trips/excursions/Hourly rates

Taxi
Leonidas Israel Quevedo (Bilingual)

+593 99 469 8332

Cuenca

Also available for day trips/excursions/Hourly rates

Azu Taxi

WhatsApp: 099-818-0192

GoGirl Cuenca

Women Only Taxi Transportation

Women Drivers – Passengers vetted

WhatsApp: 096-276-7900

Email: gogirlcuenca.ec@gmail.com

SHIPPING SERVICES

DHL Express Ecuador S.A.

WhatsApp: +593 99-9326-289

Address: Av. Alfonso Cordero 3-53 y Manuel J. Calle

FedEX

WhatsApp: +593 07-280-1965

Address: Av. Gil Ramírez Dávalos 1-156 y El Pedregal

LEGAL/VISAS/REAL ESTATE

EV Ecuadorvisas
Sara Chaca – Visa Attorney
ECU: +593 99-296-2065

USA: 1-800-655-1581
Email: sara@ecuadorvisas.com
Address: Calle Larga 6-16 & Hermano Miguel

TRAVEL

CATSA Travel Agency
Bryan Vidal
WhatsApp: 099-492-3033

Email: bryanvidal@catsa.ec
Address: Av. 12 de Abril y Jose Peralta

ORCHIDS

Ecuagenera – Orchids of Ecuador
Email: info@ecuagenera.com]
Email: sales@ecuagenera.com

Website: www.ecuagenera.com
PayPal: ecuagenera@gmail.com

CULTURAL CENTER

idiomART
Email: idiomartcuenca@gmail.com

Website: https://www.facebook.com/idiomART
Address: Mariscal Lamar 14-25 & Estevez de Toral

PANAMA HATS

TOQUILLERAS ARTESANALES DEL SIGSIG
WhatsApp: 099-499-9029

Email: atmasigsig@hotmail.com
Address: Av. Maria Auxiliadora, Sigsig, Ecuador

MAJOR GROCERY STORES

SuperMaxi
Locations: Av. De las Americas; Av. Don Bosco; Alfonso Cordero; Avenida Elia Liut & Challuabamba

Comercial Arandano súper despensa –
Bulk Food
WhatsApp: +593 (07) 246-0291
Address: Av. del Tejar 4-150

Jo Mar - Sea Food
WhatsApp: 099-562-4209 (Delivery)
Locations: Sucursal 3 Puentes; Principal Cuadra; Sucursal Estadio

ITALDELI Specialty Meats
WhatsApp: 099-445-7473
Locations: Alfonso Moreno Mora; Parque Industrial; San Sebastian

SHOPPING MALLS

Plaza Soleil – Puertas del Sol
Address: Ricardo Darquea y Rafael Fajardo
Tele: +593 99-535-2107
Restaurants, Cocktail bar, Beer Garden, Stylists, Manicures, Pet Supplies

Coral Department Store – Mall Del Rio
Address: Av. Felipe II
Tele: +593 1800267254
Website: https://coralhipermercados.com

Mall Del Rio
Address: Av. Felipe II y Cicunvalacion Sur
Tele: +593 7-281-7616
https://malldelrio.com

PARKS

Parque de la Madre
Location: Av. 12 de Abril y Florencia

Parque Calderon
Location: Mariscal Sucre y Benigo Malo

Parque El Paraiso
Location: At the fork of the Tomebamba and Yanuncay Rivers

FINANCE

Banco del Pichincha
https://pichincha.com
WhatsApp: 096 299 2999
Address: Av. Ordonez Lasso 7-182 y Los Claveles

Cooperativa de Ahorro y Credito – JEP
https://jep.coop/
Address: Sucre 10-60; enter G. Torres y Padre Aguirre
Tele: +593 07 4135000

INTERNET SERVICE

Puntonet
Av. Remigio Crespo y Guayas Esq.
Edificio San Jose
Tele: 096 336 0070 1-700-786-866

https://www.puntonet.ec

PHONE SERVICE

Claro

+593 99 1240611

contactenos@claro.com.ec

Moviestar

Locations:

Luis Cordero y President Cordova;

Bolivar Street;

Mall del Rio Shopping Center;

Remigio Crespo Street

+593 99 9001140

HOUSEHOLD/FURNISHINGS

Colineal

+593 7-280-5122

Av. Unidad Nacional y Gran Colombia

https://colineal.com

SOCIAL MEDIA

Escaping Culture

https://www.facebook.com/EscapingCulture

Young Expats and English Speakers Cuenca (#YEES)

https://www.facebook.com/groups/282164642193079

Cuenca Friends

https://www.facebook.com/groups/446065275559819

Ecuador Expats/Immigrants Uncensored

https://www.facebook.com/groups
/ecuadorexpatsuncensored/

Life in Ecuador

https://www.facebook.com/LifeInEcuador/

Cuenca High Life (News in English)

https://www.facebook.com/cuencahighlife

Cuenca Circle of Friends (Private Group)
https://www.facebook.com/groups/1394433814660296

Expats without Agendas-Ecuador
https://www.facebook.com/groups/
    CuencaExpatsSinAgendas

Cuenca Expats and Friends
https://www.facebook.com/groups/Cuencaexpats

Expats in Quito, Ecuador
https://www.facebook.com/groups/258345077546215

Good Life Cuenca
https://www.facebook.com/groups/262707778176171

Ecuador Digital Nomads
https://www.facebook.com/groups/dnecuador

Ecuador Expat Discussion
https://www.facebook.com/groups/EcuadorDiscussion

Ecuador Expats Living and Beyond
https://www.facebook.com/groups/
    ExpatsEcuadorLivingAndBeyond/

Thriving in Cuenca, Ecuador (& Beyond) for Expats and Digital Nomads
https://www.facebook.com/groups/thrivinginecuador

Expat Women Cuenca Ecuador
https://www.facebook.com/groups/301203683589234

All Artist of Cuenca, Ecuador Promote Here!
https://www.facebook.com/groups/
    CuencaArtistsofAllKinds

Yapa Tree
https://www.facebook.com/groups/cuencaexpatsyapatree

Ecuador Expats on a Budget
https://www.facebook.com/groups/1684520964896323

ESCAPING CULTURE LLC

Mary Wilson, CEO

PO BOX 1636

SUMNER, WA. USA 98390

ESCAPINGCULTURELLC@GMAIL.COM

HTTPS://WWW.ESCAPINGCULTURE.COM

www.ingramcontent.com/pod-product-compliance
Lightning Source LLC
Chambersburg PA
CBHW080837120626
46553CB00009B/2471